Pioneers of Faith

by
Lester Sumrall

Pioneers of Faith

by
Lester Sumrall

Harrison House
Tulsa, Oklahoma

Photographs in Chapters 1-10 and 12-24 are used by permission of Assemblies of God Archives, 1445 Boonville Avenue, Springfield, Missouri 65802-1894.

4th Printing

Pioneers of Faith
ISBN 0-89274-742-0
Copyright © 1995 by Lester Sumrall
P. O. Box 12
South Bend, Indiana 46624

Photographs in Chapters 1-24 are used by permission of Assemblies of God Archives, Springfield, Missouri.

Published by Harrison House, Inc.
P. O. Box 35035
Tulsa, Oklahoma 74153

Dedication

I dedicate this volume to the memory of Stanley Howard Frodsham (1882-1969): a man who loved people, a man who blessed people, a man who helped pioneer the move of the Holy Spirit in this century.

He inspired my life from the first day we met. We were together again and again in his home, his office, and in public meetings. He was present in Eureka Springs, Arkansas, when I was twenty years old, and the Lord showed Howard Carter that I was the young man to go with him around the world.

Stanley Frodsham wrote for posterity most of the challenging story that the world knows about Smith Wigglesworth. For this the Church of all time will hold him in honor. I will never forget his humility and his prolific producing of spiritual material — much of which does not have his name on it. He never received royalties, just produced fruit to bless others.

Frodsham told me when I was thirty-four years old, "You will come to know that all flesh is corrupt without Christ." I pray that the entire Church will learn this fact today.

I was never in the presence of this great pioneer without leaving with a teaching and an admonition from God's Word, and I have tried to follow his example.

Contents

Part One
Introduction

An Overview of My Journey Through the Twentieth Century

These are the last days of the Church age, I believe, and they should be fulfilling days for God's people. In order for that to happen, Christians need to understand their roots.

Our primary "Root," of course, is Jesus Christ (Isa. 11:1, 53:2), and He lives in us through the Holy Spirit. In John 15, Jesus called Himself the "Vine" and us "the branches." He is the Root, and we are His fruit. And He wants us to bear fruit for Him in our turn. He called Himself "the root *and* the offspring of David." (Rev. 22:16.)

In the closing days of this century, it is important for the Church to know the roots of the present move of the Spirit. This century has seen the mightiest moves of the Holy Spirit since the Day of Pentecost.

God said He would pour out His Spirit upon all flesh in the last days. (Acts 2:1-18; Joel 2:28,29.) At Pentecost, shortly after Jesus ascended, the Holy Spirit came in power. This move, I believe as do many others, was the equivalent of the "early rain" God had promised.

I also believe the twentieth century saw the beginning of the "latter rain" stage of God's pouring out His Spirit upon all flesh, and it has continued through move after move during the past ninety years. However, the greatest outpouring of the "latter rain" is virtually upon us.

About 1900, the world was in a state of "false peace," thinking there would be no more wars. People wanted to close the patent office, because all the possible inventions had been made. However, people were praying for revival. They thought the new century should bring revival. The entire evangelical world seemed to be praying for revival at the same time — and God brought revival.

The sad thing is that many of those praying for revival would not accept revival when it came, because it did not please them. It was not like the moves of God they had experienced before. They did not understand that what came before was a foundation, or "roots" for the next move of God.

The "latter rain" began as a tiny trickle in a Bible school in Topeka, Kansas, when a man named Charles Parham sought the Holy Spirit's gifts. Then it spread into Texas, where a black brother, William Seymour, took it to Los Angeles, and it became a full downpour.

People came to the Azusa Street Mission from all of the continents of the world. However, its greatest adversaries were fundamentalists who said they believed the Bible, yet called this move of God "heretical." They placed their doctrines that said the gifts of the Spirit were not for today above the Word of God.

The roots of the modern outpouring that began to explode into the world from Azusa Street can be found in the ministries of nineteenth-century revivalists such as Dwight L. Moody, Billy Sunday, and John Alexander Dowie, all of the United States, and Charles Haddon Spurgeon and Gypsy Smith of Great Britain. It seems to me that those revivals mark the dividing line of the early and latter rain outpourings.

Dowie died in 1907 as the Azusa Street meetings began to flow worldwide. I saw his original tabernacle. I also slept in Dowie's personal bed in the town he founded — Zion, Illinois — when I visited pioneer Finis Dake, when he was president of Great Lakes Bible Institute in Zion. I have personally experienced every move of the Holy Spirit in the twentieth century, and I have known many of the pioneers of each revival.

Just as the roots of Azusa Street can be found in the meetings of the last century, the roots of today's move of God can be found in the spiritual pioneers who lived and ministered from Azusa Street to not long after World War II.

The move of the Spirit has not stopped, nor has it even declined during this century. There are presidents and prime ministers around the world today who have the power and anointing of the Holy Spirit. A few years ago, this was not true. I have been in some of their homes, and I know what I am talking about. I have heard them speak forth in their spiritual language.

The move of the Spirit will increase until Jesus comes. This is the latter rain, and I am glad that I am a part of it.

It has amazed me to see over the years how God has found people in remote corners of the earth, brought them to the center of what He was doing in order to lay a new foundation in their lives, and then sent them back to take the move into farther and farther places.

Sometime between 1934-1936, I met Victor Plymire, a former Christian and Missionary Alliance missionary, in Hong Kong and also in Shanghai. He told me how the Lord led him into the Holy Spirit experience.

The Lord spoke to him and said, "Leave your family here and go to Los Angeles."

He asked, "What for?" but the Lord did not tell him.

He left his family on the mission field and went to Los Angeles where he received the baptism of the Holy Spirit. As a result, his denomination cut off his support.

Plymire then became a faith missionary in Tibet where he took the power of God to thousands of people in the

Himalayas. He, his wife, and children rode mules over those mountains, because they had no other way to travel. They went from village to village and preached the power of God.

When I met Plymire, he was about sixty years of age, and the anointing of God was flowing mightily through him out to others. He is typical of the early pioneers in this century who were willing to move forward with God in a new wave of the Holy Spirit.

To be like them, and to be used like them, it is necessary to know what God is doing in every move of the Spirit. Many good Christians have rejected God's new moves and, consequently, have become stagnant and missed His blessings.

Be Willing To Move With God

When I spent some years in England before World War II, I was in London and wanted to hear G. Campbell Morgan, a great preacher who belongs with the nineteenth century spiritual giants. He pastored a church that had more than three thousand people in its Bible study even in those days.

London is a very congested city, having been laid out by the Romans some two thousand years ago — and they apparently could not see straight! The streets turn and twist and are not laid out in a pattern. However, I was trying to find a big church that I thought everyone would know about.

I went up to a policeman on the beat and said, "I'm looking for the church of G. Campbell Morgan."

And he said, "I've never heard of him."

I could not believe my ears, and I said, "Why, he is world famous. He has written thirty or forty books. He is a great expositor of the Bible."

14

He said, "Well, I've never heard of him."

A passer by heard me arguing with the "bobby," and said, "Who is it you want?"

When I told him, he said, "The first door right there and to the left."

A lot of the big churches in London have a facade in front, but you cannot tell what is behind it if you do not already know.

The church was less than ten steps away, and the big cop on the beat had never heard of the pastor. If I had asked him where to find a girl, I am sure he could have told me, but he could not tell me where to get my soul fed.

The devil never wants us to get smart in spiritual things. If God sends a new breath of His power, Satan does not want us to know where it is. Or he wants us to think it must be wrong, because we "did not get it that way."

If I had lived at the time of John the Baptist, I would have joined him.

If I had lived at the time Jesus ministered on the earth, I would have joined Him.

If I had lived during the time of Martin Luther, I would have become a Lutheran because they were the ones who were carrying the banner of God.

If I had been living in the days of John Knox, I would have joined the Presbyterians, because they were carrying the flames of revival.

If I had lived in the days of John Wesley, I would have joined the Methodists, because that was where God was moving.

If I had been living in the time when the Salvation Army was founded by William Booth, I would have joined that

15

group, gone to the street corners, and "tooted a horn" for Jesus, because they were getting people saved.

I want to be where the blessing of God is being poured out. I want to be where the anointing is on people. I refuse to get stuck in some place or group where the Holy Spirit is not being poured out.

If you are not willing to move with God, then you need to understand that God is on the move and you are not. The Church needs to be on the move with God!

Why does the Lord tarry when the world looks as if it is in its final days?

There are millions in India, millions in China, and even millions in America who have not yet made the decision to accept Jesus Christ as their Lord and Savior. They are headed for hell. That is why the Lord tarries.

We need to know our spiritual roots to propagate Christianity throughout our own country and around the world.

My Personal Roots

I have been in every move of God throughout the entire twentieth century. I grew up in the aftermath of the Pentecostal move of God. After World War II, I saw the Latter Rain movement, which divided the Church in the United States. After that I saw the Healing revival, of which I was very much a part. Then I saw the Charismatic revival and the Word of Faith movement that followed. I endorsed it and became part of that flow of the Spirit of God. I am now ready for the last outpouring of God on the face of the earth.

My mother received the baptism of the Holy Spirit before I was born, so I grew up in an awareness of the Holy Spirit. I was reared in the atmosphere following the Azusa Street revival, which began in 1906.

16

My mother's roots stretched back to those revivalists of the nineteenth century. Her uncles were circuit-riding Methodist ministers. They rode on horseback from town to town, held revivals, got people saved, and founded churches. My mother was filled with the Holy Spirit after hearing the message on a street corner in downtown Laurel, Mississippi. Her acceptance of that experience changed the destiny of our family.

While she carried me in her bosom, my mother spoke in tongues every day. We grew up in the great outpouring of the Spirit of God. While other groups were running dry, we were full and running over.

In 1934, I began going to the nations of the world. I have gone to one hundred and ten nations, and I have never yet gone to a nation where the move of the Holy Spirit had not preceded me.

I do not know of another person still living who has visited with, and personally ministered for, the original pioneers of this last day revival. By the providence of God and through prophetic words spoken over my life by two British spiritual pioneers — Howard Carter and Smith Wigglesworth — I have seen what I believe to be the final outpouring of the Holy Spirit. What began at Azusa Street will, I believe, end with the return of Jesus Christ for His saints.

This book is the result of many spiritual leaders bringing to my attention that I was the last "connecting link" between the men and women who founded the "Full Gospel" churches and ministries and those who are ministering in recent moves of God. Somehow I had not become aware of this until a number of pastors, missionaries, and evangelists — widely separated from one another — began to ask me about their "spiritual heritage."

There may be other people still living who knew the Full Gospel pioneers in their own locality or nation.

However, to my knowledge, I am the last one alive who went to their countries and ministered in their churches.

Please do not feel that I am lonely, for I am surrounded at this very moment with the greatest group of young spiritual leaders ever to be on Planet Earth at one time.

I was conducting a crusade in the city of Brasilia once and staying at a large hotel overlooking the plaza filled with government buildings. Looking out the large window at what was then the new capital city, I asked the Lord, "What will my end be?"

He replied, "You will find it in Psalm 71:18."

Now also when I am old and greyheaded, O God, forsake me not; until I have shewed thy strength unto this generation, and thy power to every one that is to come.

I laughed out loud at the prospect:

I was to get old and greyheaded.

I was to exalt Christ in the Church and witness to His faithfulness.

I was to reveal His power to those who would come after me, particularly to the young ministers.

From that time onward, I had a new direction in my heart. I have gone to Bible colleges all over the world to speak to young men and women, giving my testimony of more than sixty years of proving that our God can be trusted. I can speak as David spoke:

I have been young, and now am old; yet have I not seen the righteous forsaken, nor his seed begging bread.
Psalm 37:25

In this way I have become a spiritual mentor to literally thousands of young preachers around the world. I answer their questions, I assure them of the faithfulness of God, I teach them the truths that the Lord has placed within my heart, and I do my best to pass on to them the wisdom and knowledge gained during my years in the ministry.

The faith these young men and women have in me and in my integrity toward the Lord is almost frightening. When I hear a young man with thousands of people in his congregation say that he is following me and looking to me for instruction, I realize the amazing importance of being a good mentor.

I have tried to be what the spiritual pioneer Howard Carter was to me for so many years.

I seek to bring to them what Smith Wigglesworth placed inside of me during our many times together.

As these men of another generation shaped my life, the Lord has caused me to fill this role in shaping the lives of multitudes of young ministers. My personal responsibility to these young ministers is enormous.

The ultimate example of mentors is the Lord Jesus Christ Himself.

In the nighttime I can hear young preachers say, "I have no father, no one to whom I can go, no one to love me in my day of sorrow."

It is then that I wish I were ten thousand men to embrace and instruct these spiritual leaders, for Proverbs 27:17 says:

> **Iron sharpeneth iron; so a man sharpeneth the countenance of his friend.**

What I am expressing is also true of the young Christian women in the church. Godly mothers of Israel should rise up to love them and teach them. This is so necessary at this dramatic moment in which we live.

Those Who Birthed a Global Outpouring

This book is not meant to be a detailed, general history of a very important epoch in world religion. It is meant to show the flesh and blood men and women whom God used to birth a global outpouring of the Holy Spirit — men and women in whose homes I stayed and at whose tables I ate.

I am offering a personal observation of those whose lives and ministries I witnessed who were true pioneers of a new move of God's Spirit in the earth. They are listed alphabetically to make it easier to find specific names. However, I did not meet them in this order. The first "pioneer" whom I knew was Raymond T. Richey of Texas, and the one who had the greatest influence on my early ministry was Howard Carter of Great Britain.

I am not intending to slight anyone who counts as a pioneer; however, I am only writing about the ones I knew personally. Because of the circles in which the Lord led me to minister, the majority of the people in this book were, at one time or another, connected with the Assemblies of God. I knew some from other denominations; however, I did not have close fellowship with many of them.

My personal experience with these spiritual pioneers began while I was still a child. Graham Bell, first general superintendent of the General Council of the Assemblies of God Church stayed in our home several times. In fact, our little church split when he agreed with the Jesus Only group that separated in the Twenties from the Assemblies of God.

I met the great evangelist Billy Sunday.

In Great Britain, I personally visited with Stephen Jefferys at his home in Wales, and I met his brother, George. I knew Donald Gee, John Carter, Harold Horton, and traveled with Howard Carter and Smith Wigglesworth.

I have preached in churches founded by T.B. Barratt in Norway, Lewi Pethrus in Sweden, Douglas Scott in France, and for pastors of other churches founded in those pioneer days in Australia, Great Britain, and Europe.

I knew Lillian Trasher, the great missionary to Egypt, and I wrote her life story, *The Nile Mother.*

I knew A.G. Ward, a great Canadian preacher, whose son, C.M. Ward, is still well-known in the United States.

In India, I knew Lam Jeevaratnum, a mighty worker of miracles.

These men and women impacted my life personally.

The point we need to remember today when there are so many different kinds of ministers and ministries out there, operating sometimes in ways that we do not understand, is that we all are building the same spiritual house.

As I met the pioneers of this century, who laid the foundation of the mighty worldwide revival that has ebbed and flowed since 1906, I used to marvel at their differences. They were different in natures, different in abilities, and different in ministry. Yet the Lord showed me what they all were building was *His* spiritual house.

These were the spiritual giants who pioneered remote places such as Tibet, and great cities like Oslo, Norway, and Stockholm, Sweden, along with other great metropolises of the world.

These were the spiritual giants who operated behind the scenes, such as Stanley Frodsham, an Englishman who made his home in the United States.

These "giants" were rugged, rugged people. Some were like the early apostles, who were whipped with whips and had rotten things thrown at them. They suffered for their part in putting down roots for those to follow.

These were the giants who came out of older denominations and were persecuted for becoming part of God's new move.

The saddest part of the lives of these pioneers is that most of them had such a difficult time that many of their children wanted no part of this kind of life. There was a time when I was exactly the same. The little Pentecostal church where my mother went was not very popular in town. The kids made fun of me, and even the teacher mocked and laughed.

I would come home looking terrible, and my mother would say, "What happened to you?"

I said, "It's your crazy religion! If you would just go to the Baptist church, I would get along fine. That church you belong to gets me in trouble."

Being very high-tempered, the minute we walked out of school, I would knock the daylights out of those kids and curse them. My mother, however, was determined that her children would serve God, so she never talked about persecution to us. She would read the Bible to us and pray after my father went to bed. He was not saved until later in life.

Only a few of the hundreds who started out preaching about the same time as those in this book stand out in history as "giants."

I trust this book will serve as a sort of "mentor" of knowledge and wisdom to the reader because of the foundation for revival which has been built by these twentieth-century spiritual pioneers.

Part Two
"Roots" of Today's
Spirit-Filled Christians

1

Thomas Ball Barratt:
An Unusual Servant of God
(1862 - 1940)

I visited T.B. Barratt in Norway for a two-week revival in his church when he was not quite seventy years of age. I first saw Barratt when he met Howard Carter and me at the railroad station in Oslo, the capitol of Norway. He was elegantly dressed, wearing a black hat and black top coat. He was handsome, thin and tall. His church elders also met us and welcomed us to preach in the Filadelfia Church.

During the time we were holding a meeting there, he told me how he received the infilling of the Holy Spirit and how that transformed his total being, his ministry, and his destiny.

He said that it happened when he came to the United States in 1906, although his purpose in visiting this country was to raise funds for the Methodist church, not because he had heard of any new move of God.

However, someone asked him while he was in New York, "Did you know there is a revival going on in this country?"

When he found out what was happening in California, he wrote to the mission at Azusa Street and asked how to receive the same blessing they had received from God. Their response was for him to tarry and wait on God, seeking the baptism of the Spirit daily. Also, they promised to pray for him.

He followed their suggestion, and on October 7, 1906, he received the baptism in the Holy Spirit — which marked the beginning of the Pentecostal movement in New York. Barratt, of course, took his new experience to the closest church, which happened to be a street mission. He spoke in tongues that night at the meeting, when he asked a group of people to pray for him.

Some saw a crown of fire over his head and what looked like a cloven tongue of fire at the front of the crown. Barratt said he must have spoken in seven or eight different languages that night. As a man who knew languages, he recognized the "sounds" of changing from one language to another. Then he sang in another language. The meeting lasted until four A.M.

A man named Robert A. Brown, destined to become another of the pioneers, was at this meeting, so the spark of Holy Spirit fire moved across this continent and soon was taken to Europe.

Barratt went back to Norway, called the Methodist clergy together, and said, "Brethren, I've got it."

They thought he had received a lot of money and asked, "How much did you get?"

He replied, "All I could hold."

When they said, "Tell us how much it is," he opened to the second chapter of Acts and said, "I got it. I speak in tongues."

The Bishop stood up and said, "Well, you didn't get it here," and Barratt was removed from the list of clergy!

However, he did not leave the Methodist Church for some years, and then, it was by his own resignation.

That did not stop him. He began to lay hands on people, who received the Holy Spirit by the hundreds. Revival broke out in Christiana, where he pastored a church, in meetings that were packed to standing room only. Many ministers came from all over Europe to see the phenomenon.

Among them was an Episcopal pastor named Alexander A. Boddy of Sunderland, England, who visited but did not receive. However, when he went home and preached the new message, others were filled with the Spirit — and the move of God began to move in the British Isles. England had refused to receive from the Welsh Revival a few years before, but this time, the Holy Spirit was received by many.

Boddy eventually received the Holy Spirit for himself. For years Pastor Boddy's church was the center of the move of the Holy Spirit in Great Britain. His church was like the hub of a wheel with spokes radiating out from it.

This move touched the life of Smith Wigglesworth who knew nothing about the Holy Spirit before meeting Boddy. Smith Wigglesworth and his wife then changed the world. In our generation, few men touched the world with such remarkable faith as Smith Wigglesworth.

Barratt began to take the message of the baptism of the Holy Spirit to other centers in Norway. Recently, I have been to places there where he was the founding revivalist.

Barratt was so full of excitement over the baptism of the Holy Spirit that he could not contain himself. He went into Sweden where a young Baptist preacher just struggling along heard of the great revivals in Oslo. Lewi Pethrus visited Barratt's church and received the Holy Spirit. Then Pethrus built one of the largest churches in the world.

From 1907 to 1916 Barratt was a free lance revivalist and prolific author. He published a Christian periodical in Swedish, Finnish, German, Russian and Spanish, as well as Norwegian.

Finally, he founded Filadelfia Church in Oslo, which became the largest church in Norway with more than three thousand people. He pastored that church until his death, and it is still operating today. However, it has not moved with the outpourings of the following moves of God: the healing, Charismatic, or Word of Faith movements. Instead, it has stayed with its beginning Pentecostal revelation.

The first thing that really excited me about Barratt was his piano playing. In his church he had two great pianos on the platform. His piano faced toward the pulpit, while the other instrument was placed with the rest of the musicians.

During a service, he would talk awhile, then suddenly sit down at the piano and play and sing. He was an artist of concert caliber, and I loved to hear him. I will never forget Barratt's musicianship. He would ripple arpeggios from one end of the keyboard to the other and sing some of the sweetest melodies I have ever heard.

I have never known another pastor who could play the piano so magnificently as well as sing. He was an unusual servant of God, doing an unusual work for God.

One time, he said to me, "You know, Allsummer, I like you."

I said, "My name's not Allsummer. Why are you calling me that?"

He said, "I can see in you the warmth and the light of summer, never a winter."

I responded, "Well, now, thank you, Brother Barratt. I appreciate that, but my name is Sumrall, not Allsummer."

But he said, "Allsummer — I like that!"

He is the only person who ever took me out in the snow to eat!

When I was about twenty-five years old and ministering in his church, Barratt said to me one morning, "Let's go eat breakfast in the snow."

I said, "Good! Let's go!"

We put our food in the trunk of the car and drove up into the high hills to a place he loved. We could see a dozen different mountain peaks, all snow-covered. He took out a folding table, laid our breakfast on it, and we ate in the snow. He loved nature. He loved what God had made, and he wanted to be outdoors as much as possible.

When I stayed in his home, we would talk and talk and talk about the miracles of Jesus and what Jesus did for the people. It was a joy to meet, to know, and to love T.B. Barratt. Though he died four years after I met him, he left an indelible imprint upon my life.

A Good and Faithful Servant

Thomas Ball Barratt was born in Albaston, Cornwall, on July 22, 1862. His father, a miner, immigrated to Norway in 1867. Barratt's parents and his grandfather, Captain George Ball, were faithful John Wesley Methodists.

His mother was converted at the age of eighteen, after praying for two hours, determined to know that she was saved. His father was saved when he was twenty. His family was very well-known in their community, both in religious circles and politically.

Both parents loved God with all their hearts, and built churches, as well as held meetings in their homes in England and in Norway, after they moved there. Their move came when T.B.'s father was offered the position of manager of mines for his company in Norway.

Barratt felt God's hand upon his life when he was about nine years old, but he did not accept Jesus as Savior until he

29

was twelve. He believed God had influenced his parents in their decision to choose Norway instead of a similar position in Spain, because his life would have taken a different path otherwise.

At age eleven, he returned to England for a formal education. He also attended Wesleyan College at Taunton, Sommersetshire. At Taunton, a friend led him to Christ, and a year later, a revival broke out at which about two hundred students were saved, as well as numbers of townspeople.

He returned home to Norway in 1878, where he studied art with a well-known artist and music with Edvard Greig. The same year he started a Sunday school in his home for people who worked in the mines.

In addition to his parents, he was influenced by the sermons of John Wesley and Dwight L. Moody. When he was seventeen, he read one of Moody's sermons aloud at a women's meeting his mother was hosting, and then prayed. Many at the meeting came forward for salvation.

At eighteen years of age, Barratt prepared his first sermon, after spending time in playing religious music, quiet study, and prayer. His journal notes indicate that he went up on top of a high mountain and preached this sermon to the winds.

Barratt also became active in preaching salvation in the mines where he served as his father's assistant. During this same year, Barratt shared his first extemporaneous sermon. Moody's sermons continued to serve as a foundation to what he taught, but he had no definite plans to become a preacher. He planned to be either a musician or an artist.

However, in 1882, when he was nearly twenty, Barratt passed an examination at the Methodist Episcopal Quarterly Conference, held at Bergen, Norway, to become a "local preacher." This was sort of a layman to speak to small groups and churches or to substitute for fully ordained pastors.

About this time, his recreation included translating English books into Norwegian — he spoke both languages fluently — and fighting with a bear. The bear lost, according to reports of the time! Also, he responded in writing to an attack on Methodism written by a pastor of another denomination.

Methodism at that time was still almost as controversial in some countries as Pentecostalism has been in the twentieth century. As I said, those spiritual giants who pioneered the "latter rain" of the Holy Spirit had to be rugged individuals.

In January, 1884, he preached a message entitled "Choose Ye This Day Whom Ye Will Serve," which triggered a revival that went for weeks on the mountain where they lived.

He married Laura Jakobsen in May 1887, and began to pastor a church at Christiania, where their first child was born. Barratt was ordained a deacon in 1889, and in 1891, he became an elder in the Methodist Episcopal Church of Norway. After that, he pastored several churches.

By his thirty-seventh birthday, this artist-musician who had no plans to preach, had held more than five thousand meetings.

In 1902 he founded the Oslo City Mission, and in 1904 he became the editor of its paper, *Byposten*. Both his parents had died by this time, but they must have been very proud of him long before they died.

Barratt went into Sweden, Switzerland, England, Holland, and even into India with the message of the baptism of the Holy Spirit. Thus Barratt not only founded the Norwegian Pentecostal movement, but became a key figure in the establishment of Pentecostal churches throughout Europe.

Barratt took the knowledge of the baptism of the Holy Spirit from America to leading preachers in Europe, when he could have returned to Norway and buried it. Everywhere he went, he planted the blessing of Pentecost. Directly or indirectly, he touched the lives of many other spiritual pioneers.

2

Daniel Berg

Adolf Vingren

Daniel Berg and Adolf Vingren: Men Who Would Not Compromise (1884-1963 — 1879-1933)

Daniel Berg was a Swedish Pentecostal missionary. He was born in Vargon, Sweden, on April 19, 1884. When he was about fifteen, he was saved and baptized in water through the influence of his parents who were members of the Swedish Baptist movement.

Berg's route to the mission field where he pioneered the move of the Holy Spirit in Brazil and South America was another of the Lord's involved "maneuvers" to get someone in the right place at the right time.

Born in Sweden and converted there, Berg immigrated to the United States at a time of economic depression in his home country. However, he did not receive the baptism of the Spirit in the United States. He had to return to Sweden for that.

While on a visit to his native country in 1909, Berg was introduced to the Pentecostal movement by a friend. As a result, he received the baptism of the Holy Spirit that same year. Upon his coming back to live in the United States, he met the man with whom he would minister on the mission field for some twenty years.

Adolf Gunnar Vingren was introduced to Berg during a Pentecostal conference sponsored by the First Swedish Baptist Church in Chicago. Berg had started attending several independent Pentecostal churches in the Chicago area after returning from Sweden.

He worked in a fruit shop in Chicago for one year. During that time, he received a prophecy to go to "Para" as a missionary. He did not know where Para was. Berg joined Vingren a year later in South Bend, Indiana, where Vingren pastored a Swedish Baptist Church. While Berg was there, Vingren had a prophetic dream that he and Berg were to go to "Para." However, like Berg, he had no idea where Para was.

Vingren and Berg then returned to Chicago together, where they obtained all sorts of dictionaries and atlases and learned that *Para* was a state in Brazil. Para also was the capital city of that state.

So they said, "Well, that is where we have to go to do missionary work."

In Chicago, they attended the North Avenue Mission where they were dedicated as Pentecostal missionaries to Brazil by William H. Durham.

The fare from America to Brazil was $90 for both of them, but they had to earn the money. Because of a revelation they had received on giving, they gave the first

$90 they earned to a Pentecostal newspaper. In a very short time, the Lord returned the money, and they had what was needed for the fare.

In 1910, the two men were able to travel to Brazil where Berg found a job as a foundryman. He used part of his salary to finance lessons in Portuguese (the language of Brazil) for Vingren.

Berg and Vingren did not have much success at first with their missionary work among the Baptist congregation which they had found. However, they held prayer meetings in the cellar of the Baptist chapel, where they also lived, and waited for revival.

Within a short time, a number of the Baptists began to speak in tongues. This encouraged the fledging missionaries, and they began to carry out their work with fire and zeal. However, the Baptist pastor stopped them, accusing them of being separatists and sowing doubt and unrest among the people. The pastor told Berg and Vingren to put away their "dreams and false teachings," or he would warn other missionary organizations about them.

Berg and Vingren refused to compromise. When they could no longer live and meet on the Baptist premises, they established Brazil's first Pentecostal church. This was officially registered on June 11, 1918, as the "Assembly of God." Brazil's largest Protestant body, the Assemblies of God, grew out of this church.

After Vingren's death in 1932, Berg continued to support Pentecostalism in Brazil. Two years before his own death in 1963, Berg attended the fifteenth anniversary celebration of the Brazilian Assemblies of God. Berg attended our crusades in Brazil.

The success of Berg and Vingren can be attributed to their refusal to compromise what they knew to be truth.

My connection with these two men is that the church I now pastor in South Bend is the church started by the Swedish brethren and pastored at one time by Adolph Peterson.

I was with Brother Peterson at the time of his death. We had just completed the new tabernacle in South Bend that seated a thousand people. Brother Peterson was the outgoing pastor of the old tabernacle and the first person for which we held a homecoming service in the new tabernacle.

Following Berg and Vingren, Swedish missionaries poured into Brazil, and the Pentecostal movement there is an offshoot of the Swedish movement. The Brazilian Assemblies of God is not connected with the denominations by the same name in other countries.

The "father" of Swedish Pentecostalism, Lewi Pethrus, sent many of these missionaries from his Filadelphia Church in Stockholm.

Pethrus said, "Only one missionary family to a province. Raise up a work in the capital city of each province so great that you will reach the whole state through your special Bible study groups. And once a year have a convention to bring the churches and people together."

The missionaries took his advice and the movement spread rapidly. I have visited and preached in many of these churches, those founded by Berg and Vingren and those founded by Pethrus' missionaries. I spent an entire year of my life ministering across Brazil, among tribes in the back country and up the Amazon River.

3

Fred Francis Bosworth:
A Man of Humility
and Humor
(1877-1958)

It has been good to have a direct relationship with men like F.F. Bosworth, who was born twenty-three years before the century began and who saw the days of the finalization of the early rain period in history. I did not become intimately acquainted with Bosworth on the mission field, but in my own church in South Bend.

Raymond T. Richey wrote to me in 1954 and said, "I'd like to bring a friend of mine, F.F. Bosworth, to preach for you."

I was ecstatic to think of having two people of this caliber in my church at one time.

I wrote back, "Just let me know how long you can stay and when you are arriving."

When I went to the train station to meet them, I saw two of God's unusual servants walking together. I saw an older man whom I presumed to be in his seventies. Behind him I saw a younger-looking man, but one whom I knew could not be far behind the other in age. These were men who were getting more people healed than any other two people on the face of the earth at that time.

Richey and Bosworth flowed beautifully together in speaking and praying for the sick. Bosworth usually gave testimonies from his past, and Richey laid hands on the people. They were quite a team. It was the old and the new moves functioning together. Richey came out of the nineteenth-century holiness move, and Bosworth was Pentecostal.

Our people in South Bend had never seen such men before. In fact, the city of South Bend had not had a move of God in it since the days of Billy Sunday.

At the time of the Richey-Bosworth meeting, many people in South Bend were Roman Catholic because the Studebaker Automobile Association brought people to the city from Poland and Hungary to work in the plants. Many of these people came out of their religious traditions and received the power of God in this meeting.

God discovers men in the most remarkable places and under the most amazing circumstances. He will not let these people go to third base first. He makes them go to first base, then to second base and finally to third base.

F.F. Bosworth was such a person. He became so attached to the Lord's gift of healing the sick that he wrote a masterpiece of a book, *Christ the Healer*. Still available today, this book tells of the great healing power of God and influenced evangelist T.L. Osborn in his worldwide ministry. However, Bosworth did not start out "on third base."

Bosworth was born on a farm near Utica, Nebraska, in 1877 to Burton and Amelia Bosworth. His father was a Civil War veteran. The young boy was discovered to have musical talent early in his life. When Bosworth was nine years old, he traded his cow and a calf for a cornet.

In a short time, he played the lead in the Nebraska State Band. He later led a series of twenty concerts at Madison Square Garden in New York City. Also, as part of the Lord's getting him to the right place, he led the award-winning band for John Alexander Dowie at Zion City, Illinois.

At sixteen, Bosworth and his brother, Clarence, went to see a friend, Miss Greene, in Omaha, Nebraska. Miss Greene invited Bosworth to go with her to revival meetings at the First Methodist Church. On the third night of the revival meetings, Bosworth went to the altar and was saved.

Bosworth was a "jack-of-all-trades" — a windmill factory engineer, a grocery store clerk, a cook, a butcher, worked in a car shop, was a cross-cut saw operator, a painter, barber shop owner, bank bookkeeper, bank teller, assistant postmaster and city clerk.

He once said he cooked for twenty-four boarders "and none of them died." His sense of humor helped him stay humble and handle some of the persecution that came his way. When he told the story of his life, some of the highlights were the funny things that happened to him as he tried out these various jobs.

However, something very serious happened to him while he was working at one of his many "trades." He assisted a doctor in an operation on a young boy who had been shot. The room was so warm that when Bosworth went out into the cold winter air, he caught a severe cold that developed into serious lung problems. His cough grew worse, and he lived in this condition for eight years.

Finally, doctors told Bosworth that his was a hopeless case, and he would not recover. After receiving this report, he "pulled himself together" enough to make a visit home and see his parents once more before he died. However, the Lord had other plans. On the way, he wandered into another Methodist church where a meeting was being held.

In this church, a lady named Mattie Perry told Bosworth that he did not have to die. She told him it was God's will to heal him. She prayed for him — and God healed him. Now, he was approaching "second base."

In 1906, Charles Parham, the man who helped birth Pentecost into this century, visited Zion City, where Bosworth was living at the time. Parham preached a message on being filled with the Holy Spirit. Bosworth acknowledged that Parham had something he wanted. He later admitted that he feared if he gave everything to God, He would ask him to preach.

On October 18, 1906, Bosworth was baptized with the Holy Spirit with the evidence of speaking in tongues. Bosworth's comment after he was baptized in the Holy Spirit was that he was now afraid God would *not* call him to preach.

The Bosworths Learn Faith

In 1910, Bosworth and his wife Estella moved to Dallas, Texas, where they founded a church and held nightly meetings. That church is the First Assembly of God, which he pastored for eight years. Many people were saved there and filled with the Holy Spirit. Estella Bosworth had been born a Hyde, one of the family for whom the Chicago area of Hyde Park was named.

Here, the Bosworths learned to trust God to provide for them. Many times, they had nothing in the house to eat and saw many miracles of God's providing. Their faith grew greatly through this testing.

At one time, Bosworth used his last thirty cents to buy a half-peck of wheat because of its nutritious value. His wife boiled it, and they ate it three times a day until it was gone. They found they liked it so well they bought another half-peck on purpose! After that, however, he said they never wanted any more boiled wheat.

Bosworth knew persecution as well as deprivation. In August, 1911, an annual Pentecostal campmeeting was held by black people at Hearne, Texas. They built a brush arbor off the back of the tent for white people who visited the campmeeting.

The white people who attended were impressed by the power of the Holy Spirit and the moving testimonies of the blacks. Because they did not want to seek the Holy Spirit at a "black altar," they asked the leaders of the campmeeting to call a white preacher to come and teach them about the baptism of the Holy Spirit. Bosworth was the man selected to go.

Bosworth arrived at the campmeeting at Hearne on Saturday night, August 6, 1911, to see where his meetings were to be held. He had no intention of preaching that night, but when the people recognized him, he was persuaded to preach. He spoke for a few minutes to both groups of people — the white side and the black side, standing on a platform between the tent and the brush arbor.

After the service was over, Bosworth was invited to stay that night with another white preacher. On the way to this man's room, they were stopped by a group of extreme racists who were going to kill Bosworth for "putting them on a level" with black people. Bosworth told them that he was there in obedience to God, and that the white people had asked for him to come. He also said that if God wanted him to die, he would gladly do so. The men finally allowed Bosworth and the other man to go on the condition that they would leave town immediately.

Bosworth went directly to the train depot, and the other man went back to his room to get his things. Bosworth was met at the train station by another mob of about twenty-five men. They took him from the depot, knocked him down, and beat him with heavy wooden clubs and broken boat oars. They told Bosworth he would never preach again when they were through with him.

Bosworth offered no resistance. He committed himself to God and prayed for God to keep them from breaking his spine. When the men were finished, Bosworth's flesh was like jelly, mashed to the bone covering his back all the way down to his knees. Amazingly, he only received a fracture in his left wrist.

Bosworth was not allowed to take the train from Hearne and had to walk almost ten miles to Calvert where he caught a train home the next day.

Bosworth's personal account of this story comes from a letter he wrote to his mother telling her about the mobbing. However, it tells us much more about the character of F.F. Bosworth, who had a Christ-like spirit. In his letter, he wrote:

> "The suffering during this period was terrible, but as soon as it was over, I looked away from the wounds and bruises to God, and He took away all suffering and put His power and strength upon me so that I (could) carry a heavy suitcase with my right arm over nine miles. I never had the slightest anger or ill feeling toward those men who beat me so cruelly, and the walk to Calvert in the dark with moonlight was the most heavenly experience of my life . . .

> "The Lord gave me wonderful intercession for those men that He should forgive them and prepare them for His coming . . . I have thanked Him many times for being privileged to know something of the fellowship of His suffering. Since it came for plain obedience in preaching His gospel to every creature, it has given me great joy to experience this which was so common among the early Christians in the first centuries of the church."

In 1912, the great woman evangelist, Maria Woodworth-Etter, held tent meetings at Bosworth's church in Dallas every night for several months. People were healed of serious medical problems, which attracted people to the meetings from all parts of the United States.

In November, 1914, Bosworth became a delegate to the First General Council of the Assemblies of God at Hot Springs, Arkansas. He was also appointed to a one-year term on the Executive Presbytery.

During this time and following, Bosworth became concerned about the doctrine of evidential tongues. He felt that it promoted seeking a gift instead of the Giver, that it tended to result in shallow baptisms, and that it was the source of considerable confusion. After much consideration, Bosworth decided that tongues were a gift, but not necessarily the only evidence of the Holy Spirit baptism.

A Sweet and Loving Spirit

Bosworth had many heart-breaking things to deal with during this period. His wife was in very poor health and died in 1917. He later married Florence Valentine, who survived him.

He received several letters from other ministers saying that he "had no right" to hold credentials with the Assemblies of God because of his non-belief in evidential tongues. One minister split Bosworth's church and intentionally misrepresented him to the General Council of the denomination and to his congregation. Through all of this, Bosworth's spirit still remained sweet and loving.

On July 24, 1918, Bosworth sent a letter of resignation to the Assemblies of God. In his letter, Bosworth said it was the consistent thing to do "since I do not believe nor can ever teach that all will speak in tongues when baptized in the Spirit."

Although Bosworth was no longer a member of the Assemblies of God, he was asked to go to the General Council meeting of 1918 and be on the panel to discuss the subject of evidential tongues. After discussion, a strong resolution was passed unanimously that basically stated that anyone who holds credentials with the Assemblies of God must believe and teach evidential tongues. Anyone who does not is believed to be scripturally inaccurate.

Bosworth then became a member of the Christian and Missionary Alliance. With his brother, Bert, and their wives, they carried out many evangelistic campaigns throughout the United States.

In 1919, at a meeting in Pittsburgh, there were almost five thousand reported conversions. In Detroit, in January of 1921, a woman was healed of blindness. This is one of the most dramatic healings that God performed through Bosworth's ministry. The largest crusade that he and his brother held was in Ottawa, Canada, where the building's eleven thousand seats were packed to capacity every night.

Bosworth became a pioneer in radio evangelism and established the National Radio Revival Missionary Crusaders, broadcasting over WJJD in Chicago. He had been semi-retired, when evangelist-healer William Branham began his campaigns. Bosworth not only came out of retirement to assist Branham, but was an important influence on the healing evangelists of the post-World War II revival. Bosworth's ministry was influenced by the teachings of E.W. Kenyon.

From 1952 until his death in 1958, Bosworth dedicated his life to missionary work in Africa. In one service at Durban, South Africa, he drew a crowd of seventy-five thousand people. He also held services in Cuba, Germany, Switzerland, and Japan. It has been estimated that more than a million people made decisions for Christ during Bosworth's revivals.

4

Robert Alexander Brown: Marked by Courage and Conviction (1872-1948)

Robert and Marie
Brown

Robert Alexander Brown was tall, lean, and "mean" —
and I mean that in a complimentary way! A former British
and New York City policeman, he was firm in everything
he did.

Brown was a fierce man in the pulpit, as he preached
against ungodliness, wickedness in high places, and sin of
all kinds. In his Christian work, there was no playing
around. He was a warrior, but also a peacemaker.

When you looked at his bony face, you could tell he had
been a policeman for a lot of years. When you saw that long
neck coming up off his shoulders, you just knew this was
an unusual man. Brown put a flame in me that kindled and
has burned brightly. I am so thankful God permitted me to
know him personally.

I looked at him and said, "When I am twice as old as I
am now, I can have what he has. I can have the same
determination. I can have a big work for God in a big city. If
he did it, I can do it."

He knew the streets of New York well and eventually had one of the largest Full Gospel congregations in the United States. His church, Glad Tidings Tabernacle, gave hundreds of thousands of dollars each year to missions around the world.

I had heard about him all of my life, but I first met him as a young evangelist when I was asked to speak at a Maranatha Campmeeting in Pennsylvania. Brown had his own cabin on the campmeeting grounds where he would come up to rest a couple of weeks in the summer.

When he and his wife were there, he did not miss a service that I preached. He loved the zeal in me as a young man that was similar to the zeal he had possessed years before.

Every day of the campmeeting, we had fellowship together. I learned many things from him, and I learned to love him very much. Later, I preached for him in his downtown New York church. I especially remember speaking at one of his missionary conventions. For the first time in my life, I saw tens of thousands of dollars given to foreign missions.

Later, as I traveled around the world with Howard Carter, we met missionary after missionary sponsored by Glad Tidings Tabernacle. Brown was truly a veteran and a spiritual pioneer.

He once told me a funny experience which illustrated a lifetime of courage in following his convictions and not caring what other people thought.

He had traveled to speak at a conference, and when he arrived, one of the other speakers said, "I am so tired after being up all night on the train."

Brown replied, "I am not tired. I also traveled all night by train, but I slept in a berth."

A Pentecostal preacher rebuked him and said, "Aren't you ashamed to waste God's money that way?"

Brown replied, "No! God loves me more than He does money. He would rather I arrived here rested and ready to preach than ready to go to bed."

When he told me that story, I was astonished. I had never heard anyone make such a statement. Yet, I have seen that money is not as important as the servants of God. Taking care of himself is very important for a minister to understand. Misusing the body through lack of sleep, the wrong diet, or overwork will cut short your life, and all the money you raise will not take *your* place in God's work.

We need more men like Robert Brown today — men of courage and conviction.

If I have been rebuked for any one thing in my ministry in the United States, it is that I have spoken out so strongly.

Some tell me, "Don't say things so strongly."

Then I have to explain why I am like this. When the Lord sent me back to the States, I was pastoring the great church He had me build in The Philippines, which ended up with nearly twenty thousand people. My nephew pastors this church today.

Before I turned it over to my nephew, the Lord said to me, "I want you to go back to America. You have done a good job here for Me. Go back to America now and preach *plain and strong* to the American people, because most of My servants refuse to talk hard and strong. They don't have the spirit of Hosea, Jeremiah, or Isaiah. Go and speak firm to the people of America, and I will be with you as you go."

Maybe Robert Brown looks down from heaven and smiles at me, saying, "That's my boy! He sat on my front porch for many hours, he felt my heart, and he said, 'I want to be like Robert Brown, the great pastor in New York City!'" And he would be right.

An Irishman Born to Preach

Robert Brown was born November 20, 1872, in Enniskillen, Northern Ireland, the seventh of twelve children born to Alice and Christopher Brown. Robert's mother, a woman of deep Christian character, was especially influential in his life. She prayed and taught her children the Bible much as John Wesley's mother, Susannah, did to her children.

As a strong young man with a keen mind and a restless spirit, Robert went to England seeking greater opportunities than were available in his picturesque little Irish village. In London, he joined the police force, later serving with Queen Victoria's honor guard.

His cousin, George Reid, was converted and held meetings in a Methodist church in Enniskillen. At one of his meetings while on a visit home, Robert accepted Christ. Then all of his zeal and courage became a passion to see people saved. Robert wrote the story of his conversion in a tract, "The New Birth," and more than one million copies have been circulated.

Also like John Wesley, he and two young friends were not allowed to hold services in the established churches. They met in people's homes, as did the Early Church, and also outside homes and in the marketplace.

All three of them came to the United States in April, 1898, looking for wider fields to harvest. Brown has written that he did not stop preaching on the way over, but preached on board ship. And after arriving in New York on a Friday, he preached in an open air meeting on Sunday.

His whole heart then for the next fifty years was given to the Lord's work in the States. He only made a couple of visits back home to Ireland.

Robert worked during the day on the New York police force and studied for the ministry at night. At the completion of his training, he was ordained a minister in the Wesleyan Methodist Church, with which he had been connected in Ireland.

Because of his hunger for God's best, he attended as many other meetings as possible, not wanting to miss anything God was doing. In 1907, he attended a service that was a divine appointment, if I ever heard of one.

Two young women were holding meetings at which they preached the message of Pentecost for today. At first, Brown adamantly opposed the idea that he was not already completely filled with the Spirit. Finally, however, he was convinced and sought the baptism of the Holy Spirit in fasting and prayer for three months.

At the end of this time, he fought discouragement and accusations brought to him by the devil. A short while after he withstood this strong attack, the baptism which he sought occurred.

The two young women, one of whom was named Marie Burgess, continued their Pentecostal ministry in the homes of those who wanted more of God. Because of the urgent need for a place to worship God, an empty store was acquired for services.

Robert Brown was asked to bring the opening message at this facility. His sermon, based on Luke 19:1-10, was, "Zacchaeus, Come Down!" Some forty years later, this also was his last message to the Glad Tidings Tabernacle congregation and radio audience on February 8, 1948, just before his death.

Marie Burgess wanted to be a missionary and did not want anything to be in the way if God were to call her to go. One evening, as she was praying and asking God for a definite call to the foreign field, she received a strong urge to read Matthew 19:4-6. Those are the verses in which Jesus talked about God making mankind "male and female" and a man and woman cleaving together as husband and wife.

As she read these verses, Miss Burgess realized there was a call upon her life, but she was not to be a missionary. When she returned to her room, she found six letters from Robert Brown. Robert Brown and Marie Burgess were married October 14, 1909, in Zion, Illinois. She continued to evangelize after their marriage with Robert accompanying her in most of her travels.

For fifteen years, Robert worked as a civil engineer during the day and faithfully pastored his church at night and on Sundays. The day the mortgage of $85,000 on the tabernacle in New York was burned, only four years after it was assumed, a revival began and missionary offerings were initiated. The first missionary offering was $8,000.

The Browns had promised God that if He would enable them to pay off the note quickly, they would make it a soul-saving missionary church. God did His part, and they kept their commitment. They celebrated forty years as co-pastors one year before his death.

Marie Burgess Brown took over the pastorate of Glad Tidings Tabernacle at his death and carried on the work, with the help of a nephew, for sixteen additional years. They only had one child, a son, who died at birth.

Actually, she was a better preacher than Robert, but of course no one told him so, although everyone knew it. She was a teacher, and he was an exhorter. When it came to getting people saved, he knew how to give an altar call! And, when it came to keeping people in the Christian walk, she knew how to keep them.

They made an unbeatable team for the Lord.

5

Alfred Howard Carter:
A Man of Whom
the World Was Not Worthy
(1891-1971)

The highlight of my entire life probably was the time I spent traveling and in ministry with Howard Carter of London, England. He was past forty when I met him, and I was barely twenty. In many ways, he was a delicate man. But he was also rugged, humble yet forthright and had a sense of humor that put things in perspective.

When we were traveling in Australia, a woman got her eye on me to marry her daughter. At dinner one night, she told Brother Carter it would be nice if he could be more of a gentleman like me. I stood up and left the table, I was so aghast. I came from Louisiana and from a family without a lot of money. Howard Carter was a refined, educated man from a well-to-do family.

His father was an inventor, having invented a timing mechanism that caused the bells at St. Paul's Cathedral in London to ring on the quarter, half, and full hours. His brother owned banks and theaters. In fact, when his father died, he was left quite an inheritance which he used to allow students to attend his Bible college free. But he simply smiled at this woman and thanked her. He told her we had been together for two years, and I had already helped him a lot.

He said, "With your prayers, I am sure he will accomplish the work God wants him to do in my life."

Then he came into the room where I had gone, whopping both hands on his knees — which he did when he was extremely amused — and he said, "Have you ever heard anything so funny in your life?"

He would stand up for the Bible, but he would not argue with you about anything. He never exalted himself or praised himself. You had to find out what a great person he was through the decisions he made.

One thing is for certain about him: few people understood him. Many did not appreciate him, because he would not put himself forward. Possibly he is one about whom you could say that the world was not worthy of him.

He wrote the definitive work on the gifts of the Spirit for the Pentecostal move, and his outlines are still used today.

I could go on writing down that he was this or he was that, but it would never bring Howard Carter to life for you. It would be wonderful if I could open the magic box of memory and truly bring forth the fragrance of the experiences of yesteryear. Yet all of the stories are just stories, and the flavor of the man is hard to transmit on paper.

He was a man of the Bible, and his work on the gifts of the Spirit was born in prison, while he was serving time during World War I as a conscientous objector. Officers did not understand his motive, which was not fear but conviction. And they made him work very hard and very long days.

However, great and precious things normally come after sacrifice and suffering. A pearl comes from a grain of sand lodged in an oyster's shell, creating irritation over a period of time. Diamonds come from the earth, born out of carbon and high pressure. The truth concerning the definitions and operations of the gifts of the Spirit came to

Howard Carter while he was in prison in Great Britain as a conscientous objector.

Carter was born in 1891 and died in 1971, spanning the last revivals of the nineteenth century and through the Charismatic move of this century. Born with a true gift of art but with a speech impediment, he laid both aside to become one of Britain's foremost leaders in the Pentecostal movement.

However, he always seemed to be opposed by the heirarical leaders of the movement. The traditionalists may have spoken in tongues but somehow they could not seem to grasp the supernatural. Also, many of the leaders were jealous of him. So in many areas, he was not loved and not blessed.

I saw some of the letters written to him by these people, and they were nasty. Yet he would always write back thanking them for their "exhortation" and say he would appreciate their prayers.

As a boy and young man, he could not pronounce the "r" sound; it came out as "w" — "run" became "wun" — except when he spoke in tongues. Then he could pronounce the "r" sound. This caused him much embarrassment over the years, until God did a miracle and healed him of that.

As a boy, he was deeply in love with art. His work at twelve years of age was displayed in the London Gallery of Art. He gained the highest awards for his portraiture and his life drawings. For about the first twenty years of his life, he lived, worked, and sacrificed for his art.

When he was saved and baptized in a Church of Christ at twenty, he went through a great struggle between his art and the call on his life. Eventually, like T.B. Barratt, he laid art on the altar and began to serve God wholeheartedly.

After he moved into the fullness of the baptism of the Spirit and began to speak in tongues, he had to leave his church. He was not willing to remain quiet about this experience, and the church was not willing for him to talk about it.

In 1913, the Crown Mission began in Birmingham, England. A short time later, Carter assumed leadership of the group. By 1916, a second Pentecostal work was begun. Carter was so busy with the work of two churches that he quit his job completely. However, he did not believe in asking people for money or anything else that he needed. He relied completely on God. His prison term interrupted his pastorates.

After he was released from prison, the Lord sent Carter to London to begin a work called People's Hall, or Lee Assembly. There, he met a young lady he thought would make a fine preacher's wife. As he prayed about her, God told him not to marry her. He gave Carter to understand that he would be satisfied with what God would give him. So he remained a bachelor for many years.

In 1921, shortly after this prophecy, Carter took the position of principal of the Hampstead Bible school on a temporary basis "until they found someone more suitable." However, he held that position for more than twenty-seven years. The school grew so large they had to purchase a house nearby as an annex. Two more Bible schools were opened, and Carter developed a correspondence curriculum in which students from all over the world were enrolled.

Carter was a man of very high standards. If money came into the school, he would not take it for his own use unless it was marked "personal," even if it meant he had to go without. He did not receive a salary at the school. He paid room and board just as his students did. He believed God to meet his needs, and he was never disappointed.

Howard Carter was a founding member of the Assemblies of God in Great Britain and Ireland, for which he served as a vice-chairman of the General Council from 1929-1934 and as chairman from 1934-1945.

In 1948 when Carter's position as principal of Hampstead Bible school was over, he moved to the United States where he married a widow. He then traveled widely as a preacher and conference speaker until his death in 1971.

A True Prophet of God

Howard Carter was a prophet of God. He had a book in which he kept prophecies God had given him. He allowed people to have copies of these prophecies, but I do not know whatever happened to the book. My personal experience with Carter began in a prophetic manner. I have told in other books in detail about our meeting, which was preceded by a vision God gave me.

I was sitting in a little church in Tennesee looking at the young man who was leading the music. Suddenly, the scene before me vanished, and I saw thousands of Japanese, Chinese, Indians, Malaysians, Indonesians, Indians, Africans, Latin Americans, Europeans and people from ocean islands on one road going one direction. God told me they were on the road of life that every human travels.

He said, "There is no other road. Notice, they're all going the same direction because down that road is eternity."

At first, I was excited, because I had never been overseas and had very little experience with motion pictures. I had never seen the nationalities of the world in native attire. It was very beautiful.

The Lord said, "These are the peoples of the world on their way to eternity. Would you like to see their destiny?"

He took me from my body to move above the people. As I went sweeping along, looking down on all kinds of

55

human expression, I saw all looked as if they were trying to get something. They were not walking, but almost trotting. Then I saw thousands of people as they turned and went off the main road of life.

I spoke out loud, "Oh, Lord, where are they going?"

He said, "That's the righteous. They are going into eternal life. They are leaving the road of life, and now they have entered into My life forever," which I thought was exciting.

However, when I came to the end of the "road of life," there was a precipice, and down below was a lake of fire. Instantly, I was overwhelmed with sorrow and hurt such as I had never experienced in my young life. When people got to the end of their lives and saw the lake of fire below them, they screamed, blasphemed, and tore their faces with their fingernails until blood squirted out. They pulled their hair out by the roots from the scalp. When they touched the lake of fire, there was a gentle little ripple, and they went down into it never to emerge again.

I said, "My God, that's awful, that's terrible, that's dreadful. What could You do about that?"

He said, "Seeing that you are to blame for it, I'll tell you."

How could I be to blame for Africans, Japanese, Chinese, Indians, Latin Americans and Europeans going to hell?

God quoted to me from Ezekiel 3:17,18 where he told the prophet he had made him a watchman and, if he warned the wicked, and the wicked person died in their sins — the prophet would be free of responsibility. However, if he did *not* warn them, then their blood would be on the prophet's hands.

I looked and blood was flowing between my fingers and I said, "Take it away. Take it away."

God said, "I cannot take it away."

I said, "How can You get rid of this? Why don't You tell somebody else about it?"

God said, "I have. It's in the Book, and all people will be judged by the Book of God."

Trembling and crying, I asked, "What shall I do?"

God said, "You have to go to those people."

I said, "I don't like those people. I never have seen a Japanese person in my life. I don't know those people. I cannot do that."

God said, "You have to do it, or their blood will forever be on your hands."

When I came back into awareness of the mundane life of Tennessee earth and the building, all the farmers had gone home. The young man who led the song service had gone home. There was no electricity. They took the lantern with them. The shutters over the windows were nailed together and bolted shut, so I was in total darkness. All I could see was Japanese, Chinese, Koreans and other nationalities.

I was out among the pine trees walking and praying early one morning not long after that, when God spoke to me: "Close this meeting. Go to Eureka Springs, Arkansas, to the Tri-State Campmeeting."

My sister was traveling with me at that time, so I said to her, "Leona, pack the car. Put all of our clothes in it. We're leaving right now."

When I told the pastor that God had spoken to me to close the meeting and go to Eureka Springs, he was very unhappy with me. He called me "unstable" and said he was not giving me any of the collections that had been taken during the meetings. He promised not only to never recommend me but to ruin my name as best he could with other preachers.

I said, "Sir, I must obey God."

When we arrived at the Campmeeting, we learned two foreigners were speakers. One was a German, and the other was Howard Carter from England, who spoke on the gifts of the Holy Spirit.

After the meeting I was standing on the sidewalk outside the auditorium, and as he passed by to go to his hotel, I reached out and got hold of his hand.

I said, "Sir, I will go with you over the highest mountains, I will go with you over the broad plains, I will go with you through every desert and I will go with you through the tempestuous waves of the seas. When you are old, I will succor you, love you, and bless you."

When I realized what I had said, I shook my head, and said, "Sir, I wouldn't do that at all. I don't know you and you don't know me. Would you just excuse me? I'm sorry I said these things. I want to assure you, I have never said them before."

He smiled, and said, "Come to my room."

I went to his hotel room. Carter and Stanley Frodsham, who was in his room, began talking in one corner of the room and looking through the pages of a black book. I was sure they were talking against me and were going to rebuke me for saying those silly words.

In a few minutes, Howard Carter walked over to me, and asked, "What do you think about missions?"

I said, "Oh, I love missions."

He said, "Have you ever thought of being a missionary?"

I said, "I am a missionary. I just haven't got there yet, but I am going."

When he asked me what country of the world I was most interested in, I said, "All of them. When God spoke to me, I saw the whole human race."

He said, "I prophesy and write it down in a book so everyone will know what I've said. In London almost two years ago, I was kneeling down in prayer when God told me to go to the nations of the world and teach on the gifts of the Spirit."

Then God told me, "I will prepare a companion for you. He shall come from afar. He will be a stranger when he comes, and these are the words he will say: 'I will go with you over the highest mountains, I will go with you over the broad plains, I will go with you through every desert, I will go with you through the tempestuous waves of all the seas,'" and he continued to quote all of the words I had said to him out on the street.

My eyes bugged out. I had been in the Full Gospel business all of my young life, but I had never encountered God telling a man in London and a man in Arkansas identically the same words.

Carter asked, "Would you like to travel with me? God promised me a companion. I don't know you, but God knows you, and if God knows you, that's sufficient for me. I am going to the West coast from this meeting, and I'll meet you there."

I said, "Thank you," and ran out the door.

As I drove my car as fast as I could toward home in Mobile, Alabama, where my parents had moved, I told my sister all that had happened. When I got home, I sold my car and wrote to Washington, D.C, to get a passport. However, in my excitement, I had not bothered to get Carter's address or exactly where he would be in California.

Adventures in Foreign Lands

Again, I have told in detail in other books the saga of my Holy Spirit-led trek in the footsteps of Carter to Los Angeles to Australia to New Zealand. Everywhere I went, he had told someone I was coming and to tell them where for me to go next. And, everywhere I went, I just "happened" to knock on the right door where someone had a message for me, or I just "happened" to meet the right person. God really showed me that He was in charge and that He would get us to the right place at the right time.

Then the Lord put us in the same place at the same time, and we traveled together for more than ten years in thirty countries. These travels are covered extensively in my book *Adventuring With Christ*.

Carter and I fitted together almost perfectly. He was a teacher and believed that God had sent him to the world to give the definitions and the gifts of the Holy Spirit. My ministry was evangelism, calling sinners to repentance, as well as praying for the sick. Often we used two auditoriums in the evenings to carry on the double ministry. It was very exciting to see many ministers receiving the gifts of the Spirit and many, many people being born into the Kingdom of God. It was God who supernaturally brought us together and kept us together for many years.

Some of our experiences were exalting, some were in miserable conditions, and some were humorous. For example, it was funny to see a reserved gentleman like Carter riding a mule with his feet dangling around its neck and a rope in his hand with which he was trying to make the animal move along.

We were riding on Chinese wooden saddles with no stirrups, and once the mule apparently got tired of his rider and kicked up its heels sending Carter flying down a mountainside. He climbed back up thirty feet to the road, looking the biggest mess you have ever seen. And our

Chinese guides just laughed and laughed. He did not get hurt, and we often laughed about this ourselves in later years.

In Tibet, we both grew beards, but after that trip, I quickly shaved mine off. However, he loved his "Tibetan" beard and was buried still with it. He changed the shape of it from time to time, but it was always beautifully groomed.

We really had fun crossing Russia on the border of Siberia in 1936 in the dead of winter. We did things that possibly in later years in Russia would have caused us to be incarcerated, but we enjoyed thumbing our noses at the guards sent to "dog" our every step and spy on us.

After about three weeks, we got permits to go to Moscow, because we had to get permission there to go into Poland. We were only about an hour out of town on the train when they stopped it, took us off, and brought us into a warehouse about five minutes away. They took my Bible and did not just thumb through it, but examined it page by page. Then they took off my clothes and went through them an inch at a time.

We laughed at them, but they had "iron" faces. The guards could speak perfect English we knew, because they were to listen to everything we said, but they never let on that they were hearing us. They finally let us get back on the train, but they accompanied us all the way across the Soviet Union.

The special Russian officer, who held my passport in his pocket and stood by my door on the Trans Siberian Express, even followed us to the bathroom.

I would ask him, "Do you speak English? I know you do, or you would not have been given this job."

But his face remained "frozen," and he would not even bat an eye. If I moved twenty feet away from my cabin, he followed me.

I would ask, "What town are we coming to," but he would gaze straight ahead without uttering a word to me.

Then Brother Carter would take his turn and go talk to the man outside our cubical on the train as we traveled. But he never let on that he understood a word. We also asked him if he were born again and explained what that meant. But he never even blinked an eye at us.

Even when we arrived in Moscow, he remained with us and stood by the door of our hotel room. However, Brother Carter and I lost him one night just for the fun of it. We got on the Moscow underground rail system, and of course, he followed us on. At the next stop, we suddenly jumped off without giving him any indication we were going to do that. He was unable to get off the train fast enough to follow us.

After that, we wandered the streets of the city unaccompanied. When we returned to our hotel, there stood our guard, gazing straight ahead, giving no sign that he had to have been greatly embarrassed about us slipping out of his surveillance.

I said, "Good night!" But he still did not reply or give any indication that he understood me.

You might not think two preachers would do things like that, but Carter had a odd sense of humor that made life very interesting.

The last time we were together after he married, he said, "Lestah," (that is how "Lester" sounds in a British accent), "Never marry a widow, because the greatest man who ever lived just died!"

In Inland China, a sense of humor stood us both in good stead. There were no bathrooms and not even any outdoor toilets. You had to use the open range, and women would come out of town and think nothing of going to the bathroom right beside you.

The only toilet paper we had was newspaper. Never having experienced this kind of thing before, I knew no "protocol" for a strange woman going to the bathroom right next to you! The first time it happened, I just handed the woman next to me the newspaper pieces I had left over. She seemed very pleased, because it probably was the first time she had used paper. However, she had watched me and knew what to do with it.

I walked away shaking my head and thinking how very different in traditions and cultures all the people traveling down the road of life are — and, yet, how much the same we all are in needing Jesus Christ as Savior.

In Japan, the way you took a bath in pre-World War II days was to heat a lot of water in a large barrel, then dip out of it into a smaller tub. However, I thought a bathtub was a bathtub, so I climbed into the bigger vessel and lathered myself up with soap the first time we stayed in a home. Then I noticed the water was getting warmer with steam coming up from it.

I said, "They are trying to cook me in here!"

I climbed out and looked underneath the tub, and there was a little furnace under there. I had contaminated the entire water supply of the whole family that had to take baths that day.

I told Carter, "When you go for a bath, be careful. Don't get into the big tub, because that is where they boil you. You will never live to tell the story if you climb into that big wooden barrel."

We were in Java for more than three months and traveling conditions were very primitive. We went third class on third-class trains. The aisle was piled four or five feet high with all kinds of bags and sheets with people's possessions tied up in them. The windows had no glass, just shutters, which you had to let down to see outside.

However, the engines were fired by wood, and cinders flying back would be blown into the windows. They would burn your clothes, if you did not watch out for them.

Some of the more elegantly dressed passengers wore little white jackets, which we found was to protect them from the dust and debris of the journey. They could take them off when they got there and still look decent. However, we had no little white jackets, so when Carter and I arrived, we looked as if we had been in a furnace of some kind.

This one day, the train was packed, and Carter sat on one side, and I sat on the other. I got a window seat, which I thought was good — until I began to get so dirty. Next to me was a man who must have been a Christian, although we did not speak one another's language, so I do not know for certain.

However, when he got ready to eat his lunch, he closed his eyes, put his hands to his chin, and began to say grace. He had such a nice lunch that it made you hungry to look at it. What he did not know was that the man across the aisle had a monkey. When he closed his eyes to pray, that monkey jumped across and grabbed his lunch, bag and all. Then he ran to the top of the train and sat up behind some luggage, peeping out to see if he was being chased. That poor man did not get any of his lunch.

I did not know whether he could understand me or not, but I leaned over and said, "Sir, the Bible says to *'watch* and pray.'"

The man was pretty upset, but the one who owned the monkey never said a word or did anything about it.

On this trip, we had our first experience with demon power. At a kind of junction with a store and a few houses, there was a naked man fastened to a pole with a rope tied around his neck and another around his foot. He was like an animal and would run growling at the people, who poked him with a stick to make him act wild.

That was my first time to see real demon possession, and the spectacle has stayed with me all of the days of my life. I always have had such compassion for those tormented by demons. Eventually, God led us into dealing with demons on people.

In all of our travels to strange places and amid strange cultures, this refined British gentleman was the perfect companion. I could not have had someone my own age who would have been any better to minister with through bad times and good.

Carter taught on the gifts of the Holy Spirit, but he did not function in all of the nine gifts. We flowed together in ministry as if we were one, although as a Britisher and an American, we could not have been more different. He taught on the gifts, and I gave the altar calls and prayed for the sick.

Howard Carter actually knew God similar to the Old Testament prophets. He was more in the nature of an apostle, but he also was a prophet. His prophesies, written down and given to people, sometimes with an exact date, always came true.

We traveled together for a great number of years, and all the things I had said to him supernaturally the day I first met him came to pass. He went to be with the Lord in 1971 at eighty years of age. He possibly blessed and touched my life more than anyone else. It has grieved me to this day that I was unable to preach his funeral because of a severe snowstorm that closed all the airports.

6

Finis Jennings Dake: A Pioneer in the Word of God (1902-1987)

Finis and Dorothy
Dake

Dr. Finis Dake was one of the best friends I have ever known. I met him when he was president of the Great Lakes Bible Institute in Zion, Illinois. The school later moved to Minneapolis and is known today as North Central Bible College.

Dake had secured the premises of John Alexander Dowie's home and carriage house for the Bible College. He used the giant stables where Dowie kept his horses and carriages for the dining area and kitchen and used the magnificent old home for classrooms and offices. Dake loved that spot.

When you met him, you saw a man whose eyes were red, and you would wonder, "Why are his eyes so red?"

He would timidly say, "Well, I haven't been to bed in two days. I have been working on annotating the Bible."

I can see him now, me looking over his shoulder, books stacked at least two feet high on every side of him, working away late at night writing his giant Bible that is now sold all over the face of the earth. He had a very large body, not fat, not heavy, but strong. He was a big man.

He said to me when I was first there, "Lester, I am going to do you a great favor. I have had the ladies prepare Dr. Dowie's private bedroom for your stay. You will actually sleep in the bed where he slept. I have never let anyone sleep in that bed. You will be the first to do so since Dowie died."

Dake loved that place more than any other place he lived in his entire life.

He took me to the basement and showed me an enormous concrete vault as large as a bedroom that Dowie had built before there were any banks in the city of Zion which he founded. On the walls were shelves: one for $1 bills, another for $5s, another for $10s, and so forth. The coins were stored in wash tubs. In those days, you could buy practically anything with a penney. Dowie was almost like King Midas in the fairy tale, surrounded with "gold." Dowie had a lot of money, but he lost the reality of God's calling on his life.

The world knows that in his latter days, Dowie lost his church and was confused regarding his ministry. However, in his heyday, Dowie did marvelous things for God. He had Zion City carved out of the wilderness. The original tabernacle seated two or three thousand people. The ceiling was rather high, and the walls of that entire vast auditorium were lined with crutches, walking canes, medical paraphernalia, and all kinds of things.

When you walked in there, you thought you had entered another world.

I asked the custodian, "Do you ever add any crutches?" I could see there was no room, but I asked anyway.

He said, "Oh, no! We would not ever add anything to Dr. Dowie's collection."

I said, "Do you ever get anyone healed here?

"No," he said, "there is no one sick around here anymore. Dr. Dowie healed them all."

I could see they needed another custodian who knew people were being healed everyday, one who knew there still were people who needed God's power.

However, I probably am one of the few people still living who saw those four walls full of leftovers from the mighty power of God. Years later, I revisited the site, after everything had burned to the ground. All of those evidences of God's miracle-working power had been destroyed.

I lectured to Dake's students for several days having just returned from Germany and Russia where I had seen the gruesome Nazi and Communist regimes destroying humanity. The students were especially interested in prophecy. He also pastored a church in the city, and I spoke there several nights. We were together constantly on this visit.

He told me it had taken a hundred thousand hours to write the notes for his Bible. I saw the office where he worked. He taught in the Bible school by day, and after dinner each night, he would work on his Bible, often working all night long.

He was a different kind of pioneer, a pioneer in the Word of God. He learned Greek and Latin by staying up all night. He could tell you the true meaning of every word in the Bible and give you the opinions of various scholars.

When we opened our church in South Bend in 1967, Dr. Dake was one of the first spiritual pioneers to teach in our Bible seminars. He came at least once a year to teach our people.

A Gift of Memory

Born in 1902, Dake was born again and baptized in water at seventeen. Until then he had rejected Christianity because of what he thought were the hypocritical attitudes of the Christians he knew. However, he finally met some Christians who lived what they preached. Then he chose to surrender his life to the Lord.

He continued to cry out for a closer walk with God after being born again. Three months later, in May, 1920, Dake received the baptism of the Holy Spirit. He described this as a "cool and rushing wind" flowing over his body and said it seemed that he could hear the fluttering of the wings of a dove.

Immediately, Dake said that he became aware of an ability he did not previously possess. He could quote Scripture verses by the hundreds, although he had read little of the Bible up to that time. This was a definite gift from God, as his wife testified to his poor memory in other matters!

After attending Central Bible Institute, Dake was ordained in the New Mexico-Texas district of the Assemblies of God when he was twenty-four years old. He and his wife then lived in Amarillo, Texas, where he pastored.

In college, Dake made a vow to God that he would never teach one thing in private or in public that he could not prove by the Bible. He also vowed never to change what the Scripture says.

Dake served as an evangelist from 1928-1931 during which time he lived in Tulsa and Enid, Oklahoma.

Dake authored several books, tracts, and pamphlets, although he is best known for his *Annotated Reference Bible*, first published in 1960. Together with his wife Dorothy, the notes for this Bible were compiled and edited over a seven-year period.

One night at my church in South Bend, to everyone's amazement, he began to quote verbatim the entire book of Revelation from memory. With the congregation following line by line, we were amazed as he went straight through the entire book.

At one point he smiled at the people and said, "Would you also like the punctuation?"

He was challenged once by a local preacher on whether or not he could quote the New Testament verbatim. Dake agreed to sit behind a glass window in a large department store and do this, providing the local radio station would put his entire quotation on the air. The station agreed, and Dake quoted the New Testament from Matthew to Revelation without opening a Bible. He gave the number of each verse and indicated chapter changes.

In 1932, he was called to pastor Christian Assembly in Zion, Illinois. A short time later, he bought the Dowie home and carriage house. In 1937, however, he served six months in jail after pleading guilty to violating the Mann Act. He had transported a sixteen-year-old girl across state lines, registering as man and wife. Dake swore nothing wrong occurred, and his lawyer called it "an unfortunate mistake."

He told me that he had passed this girl hitchiking along the side of the road in winter time. He gave her a ride and talked to her about his college. She was a runaway, belligerent toward her parents and toward school.

He said, "Now, I *knew* better than to pick up a girl hitchhiker, although I was three times her age. But I didn't act on my better judgment. I took her with me, feeling sorry for her, and thinking I could turn her life around. I fed her in restaurants.

"As soon as I let her out of my car, however, she called her parents in Illinois and laughed in their faces. She told them a real handsome man with a beautiful face gave her free transportation all the way to St. Louis. When they got my name, they immediately took out a warrant."

His wife and his church remained loyal and supported him all through the succeeding embarrassment; however, he was released from the Assemblies of God. Later, he joined the Church of God of Cleveland, Tennessee, and then eventually became an independent. Through his annotated Bible, his impact on the Pentecostal movement was tremendous. About thirty thousand copies of his Bible still sell each year.

Again, God brought good out of what the devil meant for evil. In jail, Dake had time to finish that Bible, just as Carter had gotten the basic revelation and outline on the gifts of the Holy Spirit in jail. The classic Christian book, *Pilgrim's Progress* came out of John Bunyon's time spent in prison.

Most of us want blessing without suffering, but if there had not been a cross, there would have been no resurrection.

After Dake's retirement to a home in Georgia, I went to visit him several times. He had in his mind to build a giant concrete Noah's ark on his land the same size as the original, but he never did it.

The last time I visited Dake and his wife, it was very sad. Both were confined to wheelchairs. She had arthritis, and he had suffered a stroke and could not speak clearly. As he showed me around the great printing room where thousands of Bibles were continuously being shipped out, tears ran down his face as he reminisced about our friendship from 1939.

He smiled and cried and held on to me, this man with the high forehead and a face like a prince. I recognized him for the mighty giant he was mentally and spiritually. He will long be remembered as a man of the Book.

7

Stanley Howard Frodsham: His Pen Was Tuned for Greatness (1882-1969)

I met Stanley Frodsham for the first time in the hotel room with Howard Carter in Eureka Springs, Arkansas, when God first put Howard and me together for our missionary journeys. But I only became intimately acquainted with Frodsham several years later in Springfield, Missouri, at Assemblies of God headquarters.

He edited the *Pentecostal Evangel* for nearly thirty years and wrote fifteen books. His office was very humble, although as editor-in-chief, he could have had any office he wanted. However, he was a very humble man. He did not look as if he weighed more than a hundred and twenty-five pounds with his little bald head and great big smile.

Every time I visited him, he gave me a new perspective on the human heart, the Adamic nature in rebellion against God. He would sit and cry while he talked of this and say, "Remember the will of man is the biggest hindrance to God."

He said we must be servants who do not choose our destinies and do not choose the things we want to do. We must choose Jesus, and He chooses our paths through life. It was always a learning time when you went into his office.

Young preachers always were given a welcome in his office. He wanted to show them how to be great, although he himself was not a very effective speaker. However, his pen was tuned for greatness.

He Let Jesus Choose His Path

A native of England, Frodsham attended a private school in Bournemouth, until he was fourteen. In later years, because of his interest in writing, he studied at a private school in England.

Frodsham was converted in the Young Men's Christian Association and then spent a year in Johannesburg, South Africa, as the secretary for the newly formed YMCA. In 1908, Frodsham received the baptism in the Holy Spirit at Alexander Boddy's All Saints Church in Sunderland, England, which had become the hub of Pentecost in Great Britain.

With his wife Alice Rowlands Frodsham, he immigrated to America in 1910. In 1916, he was elected general secretary of the General Council of the Assemblies of God. In 1917, he became the missionary treasurer, and in 1921, he was elected editor of all Assemblies of God publications. He also wrote for Sunday school papers and quarterlies.

Of the fifteen books Frodsham wrote, the best known is *Apostle of Faith*, a biography of Smith Wigglesworth. I believe his greatest achievement was when he obeyed God, Who put it on his heart not to let the works of Smith Wigglesworth die, and wrote that book. If it had not been for this dedicated man, the world would never have known much about Smith Wigglesworth.

It has been said that Frodsham's contacts with the Pentecostal movements in Europe and across Canada gave the early editions of the *Evangel* a broader perspective than most Pentecostal publications. Assemblies of God leaders felt the *Evangel* kept missionary enthusiasm at a "boiling point."

In 1949, Frodsham retired as editor of all Assemblies of God publications and gave up his credentials. He then ministered for several years in the move called Latter Rain and taught for a season at Elim Bible Institute. While at Elim, a prophecy was given about praying for Argentina. Frodsham took a special interest in Argentina after that.

From 1950 on, his counsel and ministry were sought after because of his depth of experience and his ability to inspire others. Frodsham was a spiritual father to many.

He told me often how a young man should live and grow spiritually to achieve more than man looks upon as "normal." He, truly, was a great man.

8

Donald Gee: Ambassador-At-Large (1891-1966)

Another Britisher whom I knew from those early days was Donald Gee, a true spiritual aristocrat. He could walk into a group of ministers, and immediately, they would feel him a leader in their midst. He could go to a general conference unannounced, and before you knew it, he would be on the platform preaching.

On the other hand, in private life, he was of a shy and retiring nature, seeming aloof and almost austere.

He had a compelling way about him and a constant smile that was all his own. It was not quite a grin, yet it made a place for him wherever he went. Anytime you saw him, every hair was in place. The knot in his tie was exactly where it should be, and his clothes were immaculate.

His face stayed red as catsup almost all of the time, but he was not embarrassed. It would have been hard to embarrass him. He was a master of the clever answer.

He so often said, "What we need is balance," that he became known as "the apostle of balance." He avoided extreme positions within the Pentecostal movement. He knew how to handle an embarrassment and not hurt anyone. Whatever argument came up, he did his best to be a part of the answer.

I studied him very, very carefully. If he was in a convention, and a storm was brewing about a doctrine or something, he would sit there smiling all the way through.

And if someone asked, "Brother Gee, do you have a word about this?" he would answer, "Isn't it wonderful that they are both right? Isn't it just wonderful? Of course, both of them are leaning a little bit to the edge of the road, and they ought to pull back to the center. Then they would be *more* right than they are now."

Because of his habit of not being controversial, he stayed in the middle of the road, while not being too much of a compromiser. He did his best to be at least a little part of the answer when an argument arose, not part of the problem. You could call him a "peacemaker."

Gee's teaching was very simple, very well-organized, and very well-thought-out. He was a thinker. You might also say that he was a friend of pastors throughout the world. His books were translated into many languages. He was a teacher, not one who prayed for the sick. When he finished his messages, he would quietly turn the service over to someone else.

Once Donald Gee was baptized in the Holy Spirit in England, he led a more interesting life overseas than he did at home. He would come to America two or three times a year, Canada once or twice, Australia, New Zealand, India and the Orient. He spoke in every large Full Gospel school, and he spoke to all denominations that would have him.

I never had a lot of fellowship with Donald Gee. I was close to him, but he knew Howard Carter was my mentor. Gee and Carter were reared together spiritually in the fundamentals of faith. However, he sometimes had strong words with Carter, who would not answer back. And, when they met, they were close friends. There was a deep appreciation in each of their hearts for the ability of the other to bless humanity in our day. When Carter gave up the principalship of the Bible college at Hampstead, he put Donald Gee in that place.

I did enjoy sitting with him on a platform from time to time and watching him grin even when he did not like something. That smile gave him an acceptance among lay people.

They would say, "Look at that happy man. Donald Gee is a happy man."

Gee was a pastor, author, educator, conference speaker, and editor. He also was a well-qualified musician and often asked to play the piano or the organ for meetings. In fact, he produced the first *Redemption Tidings Hymn Book* in 1924 and began contributing articles to Pentecostal periodicals that same year.

The Apostle of Balance

Born in London, England, on May 20, 1891, Donald Gee accepted Christ in 1905 at fourteen years of age in a Congregational church. In 1913, Gee joined the Pentecostal movement. He also married in 1913.

Like Howard Carter, he too spent time during World War I as a conscientious objector. He worked on a farm, however, not in prison. Until he began to pastor, he earned his living as a sign painter.

In June of 1920, at the age of twenty-nine, Gee became a pastor of a chapel in Leigh, a suburb of Edinburgh, Scotland. Because he began his pastoral duties in Scotland, he was especially revered there.

In 1921, Gee attended the International Pentecostal Conference in Amsterdam, his first involvement with the larger Pentecostal movement. He had quickly embraced the desire and need for a world Pentecostal fellowship. Gee became a world pioneer teacher of the Word of God. He was an "ambassador at large" for the Full Gospel work.

He was one of the fifteen foundation members of the Assemblies of God in Great Britain in 1924 and served on the group's executive council for forty years. In 1928 Gee left England to serve as a Bible teacher in Australia and New Zealand for seven months. On the way to this assignment, he wrote his first book, *Concerning Spiritual Gifts*. Despite being a self-educated man, he wrote some thirty books in all.

Gee lectured all over the world until World War II when his travel was restricted. He traveled on all five continents, visiting at least sixty countries.

Gee was elected and served as vice-chairman of the British Assemblies of God from 1934-1944 and served as chairman from 1945-1948.

In 1947, Gee accepted the invitation of the first world conference in Zurich, organized by David du Plessis and himself, to found and edit *Pentecost*, a magazine that carried a review of revival and missionary news on a worldwide scale. He held this assignment from 1947-1966.

In 1951, Gee accepted an invitation to become principal of the Assemblies of God Bible College at Kenley, Surrey, England. Gee was world famous as a Bible teacher, which no doubt attracted many students to the Bible school. It was constantly full under his leadership.

Gee's wife Ruth died in 1950. They had three children. He remarried less than a year and a half before his death.

As for himself, he died of a heart attack in a taxi as he rode home from the funeral of one of his best friends. For him to meet the Lord with four wheels rolling underneath him was a normal thing for him to do. As a traveling man, he went to the corners of the earth teaching the truth of Jesus Christ, so maybe it was appropriate for him to go to heaven from a taxi!

9

Willis Collins Hoover:
Father of Pentecostalism
in Chile
(1856-1936)

Born on July 20, 1856, in Freeport, Illinois, to Methodist parents, Willis Collins Hoover pursued the professions of medicine and architecture. In 1884, he repeatedly received what he called a strong inner impression, "South America. . . South America . . . South America."

When Hoover realized God was calling him to the mission fields of South America, he told the Lord he would go as soon as he paid his debts and found a wife. In 1888, Hoover married.

Hoover went to Chile as a Methodist missionary, received the baptism of the Holy Spirit and founded the Pentecostal movement in Chile. He raised up one of the largest evangelical groups in Latin America.

Although he had no formal training in theology, he gained an appointment in 1889 as rector of the Iquique English School in Northern Chile under the quasi-independent mission of Methodist bishop, William Taylor. He soon began his studies for ordination.

From serving a small Spanish-speaking congregation in Iquique, Hoover was promoted to superintendent of the Iquique District when Chile was divided into three areas in 1897 and appointed pastor in Valparaiso, the largest church in the conference in 1902.

Hoover expanded his evangelistic thrust to include branch chapels, class meetings, house-to-house visitation and cottage meetings. He kept up with the activities going on in the Church worldwide as much as possible. He read about Evan Roberts (1878-1947) in Wales and A.B. Simpson (1843-1919) in the United States.

He learned of the Pentecostal outpouring in India through the book of his wife's former classmate. *The Baptism of the Holy Ghost and Fire* by Minnie F. Abrams told of a revival among the widows and orphans in a school and home operated by a high caste Indian where Miss Abrams was then working.

After reading this book, Hoover asked others about the Pentecostal outpouring, which, with the exception of tongues, differed little from the emotional expression of pioneer Methodism. It was during this time that Hoover and his wife also heard from a friend in Oak Park, Illinois, who had experienced the baptism of the Holy Spirit with the evidence of speaking in other tongues.

Hoover's Pentecostal activities and those of Nellie Laidlaw, a new convert and prophetess he had endorsed, cost him the superintendency but not his pulpit at the 1910 conference in Valparaiso. However, effective May 1, 1910, Hoover resigned from the ministry and membership of the Methodist Episcopal Church, taking most of his own and two other congregations with him. He reorganized his congregation into what he called Iglesia Methodista Nacional, which experienced extensive growth.

When this movement split in 1932, Hoover established the Iglesia Evangelica Pentecostal de Chile, which he headed until his death four years later.

When Hoover built his first church in Chile which would seat twelve hundred, his congregation at that time numbered less than five hundred.

He often prayed, "Lord, do not let this building mock us. We are building it to save sinners. Thou must fill it," according to his own writings.

Hoover's work was not without opposition from Christians and co-laborers as well as unbelievers. Newspaper headlines called him "The Great Impostor," "hypnotist" and "suggestionist." The public slander against the baptism of the Holy Spirit was severe, so he knew this persecution was not personal but for the Word's sake.

In the year following Hoover's separation from the Methodist Episcopal Church, his congregation added one hundred and fifty new members. Board members and some congregational members left Hoover's church to begin new works, thus multiplying Hoover's influence.

Not only were people being baptized in the Holy Spirit, but supernatural healings were taking place. People were healed from smallpox and delivered from insanity, for example. However, Hoover's primary focus remained on the transformation of lives.

Tried and tested on the mission field, Hoover and his wife became ill with typhoid fever. Also, they went through a smallpox epidemic where fifty to one hundred people died daily, and they lived through an earthquake. More than two thousand people were killed in the earthquake, but Mrs. Hoover was able to rush home from a prayer meeting and get their children outside just before the roof fell in.

Hoover translated hundreds of hymns into Spanish, which are still in use today. He was an apostle of Pentecost to an entire nation.

10

Harold Lawrence Cuthbert Horton: Defender of "Initial Evidence" Doctrine (1881-1969)

One of the most exciting persons I met on my world tour of many nations was Harold Horton. At the time we met, he was a teacher at Howard Carter's Hampstead Bible School in England. He lived just down the road from where he taught.

I would visit him at his home in the afternoons and evenings and found that he had a very remarkable mind in conceiving new things and the ability to share them with one half his age. We had perfect fellowship and joy together. He would hit his knees with both hands, as we laughed about his giving up his professorship at one of England's world-famous universities to teach in a Full Gospel Bible college.

Members of Parliament, ministers, and actors were among his elocution students. He loved the English language and spoke in torrents of trained eloquence. Horton later had just as illustrious a career in Pentecost. We became very close during my time in England. Although he never boasted of his achievements, I gained a wealth of information from him.

Horton was born in Wrexham, North Wales, only five years after Stephen Jeffries was born in South Wales. He was brought up in the Methodist tradition by godly parents and trained as a Methodist minister. He was converted to Pentecostalism when one of his pupils took him to a Smith

Wigglesworth service where he was healed of a double hernia.

He immediately threw out his old sermons and began to study preaching all over again, now that he had found out that miracles are for today as well as for the day of the disciples.

After Horton met Carter, he was very instrumental in getting Carter's notes on the gifts of the Spirit in shape to publish. Horton was particularly influential in the development and defense of the doctrine that the initial evidence of the baptism in the Holy Spirit was speaking in tongues. This affected the Assemblies of God in Great Britain and Ireland, as well as in the United States

Horton became a well-known pastor, a prolific author who contributed to most English-language Pentecostal periodicals, as well as a teacher. Because of his enthusiasm concerning the baptism of the Holy Spirit, he was known affectionately as "Hallelujah Horton."

11

Lam Jeevaratnam[1]:
A Messenger of Jesus

Some of the mighty and unusual pioneers of this century lived in remote places of the earth. If you did not travel, you would not know about them. For example, an Indian named Lam Jeevartnam was an extraordinary man, one of the most remarkable people I have met worldwide.

I felt I knew him very well after meeting him in England on several occasions and getting to know his background and his ministry in India. Jeevaratnam always dressed in traditional Indian clothes. When I met him, he had a long beard that was mostly white. His hair was gray mixed with white. He was a very kind and gracious man, who looked mature, yet still very strong.

From the world to the ministry, Jeevaratnam gave up everything of earthly value and began preaching the Gospel with signs and wonders following. He had gone to England to make money as an artistic entertainer, but God's plans prevailed. He was saved in an open-air meeting in Leeds, then went to Howard Carter's Bible school where he was baptized in the Holy Spirit.

In Jeevaratnam's meetings, the dumb spoke, the ears of the deaf were opened, the lame walked, severe internal pains vanished, and the blind received their sight. In his meetings, it was obvious that Jesus has all power over the enemy, and He has invested that same power in believers.

---

[1]Photograph and dates were unavailable.

Jeevaratnam had an unusual discernment of the presence of demon power and the knowledge of how to deal with it. In India, he was often called "Lam, the devil chaser," because he stayed with his calling, which was a mighty deliverance message that Christ is the answer to human needs.

He dominated demons in a very strong manner until anyone could tell there was no fear in him, because demons ran from him.

He lectured and spoke some in England during his life, but his greatest work was among the villages of India. There are more villages in India than anywhere in the world, except China. They grow their own food, live their simple lives, and die unknown to, and mostly unknowing of, the world in which Western Christians live.

He had to stay on the move from one of these villages to another, and we are talking about perhaps a hundred thousand of them, in order to stay out of the way of the Hindu officials. They would like to have killed him.

I am sure we looked like two funny "ducks" walking down the street together or into some of the churches where we ministered together — him with a beard and in the long Indian robes and me dressed like a young Englishman.

Jeevartnam held a tremendous revival once in Poona City. The revival was held outdoors to accommodate the masses of people attending. People from numerous sects and denominations came — from Hindus to Mohammedans, Brahmans, outcasts, Parsees, Jews, Sikhs, Panthans, Roman Catholics, to name a few. Rich and poor and high and low caste sat together listening to the full Pentecostal Gospel preached by Brother Jeevaratnam.

The missionary sisters and young Indian men and women helped control the crowds of sick people who came for prayer. Similar to the days of Jesus' earthly ministry, people climbed surrounding walls and looked on from balconies of houses and tree branches. Perhaps thousands of people heard the gospel preached through Brother Jeevaratnam.

We ministered together in several convention meetings. At one of the conventions, we stayed in the same house. He told me many of the stories of the functioning of demon power in India.

One story he related has remained in my mind through the years. He was walking to an appointment one evening and about twenty steps in front of him appeared the most beautiful Indian girl wearing a sheer see-through gown. She smiled at him, beckoning him to come to her.

He answered, "No, I cannot! I am a man of God, and I am on my way to preach."

The girl kept moving toward him, begging him to come to her. He repeatedly said, "No!"

After a few moments, the Holy Spirit spoke to him, "This is a demon and not a person. If you give in to this demon, you will be possessed."

Brother Lam stopped, raised up his hands and cried, "Oh, the blood of Jesus, save me from this demon."

He then shouted, "Go, in Jesus' name!" Instantly the girl disappeared.

Lam looked for her behind the trees and in the high grass. He went to a couple of houses, described her and asked, "Have you seen a beautiful girl around here?"

The people of that area were humble farmers and told him that no girl of that description lived in their village.

Lam warned me as a young preacher to "always resist even the appearance of evil. In doing so, evil will never subdue you. The blood of Jesus is the answer."

He was known as "a true son of India, but a messenger of Jesus."

12

Stephen Jeffreys

George Jeffreys

Stephen and George Jeffreys: Two Brothers With Sad Endings (1876-1943 — 1889-1962)

Stephen and George Jeffreys were born in a small village in Wales. Since Wales at that time was world famous for coal, their father and all of their relatives were coal miners. However, the Jeffreys were religious people, open to know more about God and to grow spiritually.

What started Stephen down the path of becoming one of the most unusual ministers of the entire twentieth century was a vision that appeared in their church in Wales. This vision involved a bleeding lamb. About three hundred people came to see this phenomenon.

Stephen was so fascinated by it that he lay down on the floor under the vision and cried out to God for three days about the needs of the world, especially physical healing for people.

He felt the anointing of the Lord come upon him. And when he left the church building, he found that when he prayed for people, they were miraculously healed. Within a short time, any building he rented was immediately filled to overflowing. In some cities, people would stand in line as long as three days to get into the building.

Stephen Jeffreys was a man of iron. He would sing and preach and pray for the sick, then go to a nearby hotel and eat and sleep for two or three hours. During that time his workers cleared the auditorium, got everyone out, and opened the front doors. No one paid attention to whether it was 11 at night or 2 in the morning. After two or three hours of rest, Stephen would come back and repeat his singing, preaching, and praying.

In the middle of a service, Stephen would jump off the platform, run to the back, curse rheumatoid arthritis, for example, and scream, "Come out of him."

People said you could hear bones pop for approximately thirty feet around as the person's bones began to relocate.

Howard Carter told me of being in the auditorium one night whan a young man came along with one leg that just dangled, because it had never grown.

Stephen Jeffreys put him on the platform and said, "Leg! I tell you, grow, in Jesus' name!"

Thousands of people watched as that young man's leg grew out eighteen inches. Carter was a very conservative man in a country of conservative people. However, he said the people went berserk.

He said, "Brother Sumrall, they did everything except stand on their hands. They jumped. They ran. They screamed!"

When people are healed through prayer, it is sometimes very difficult to stay humble, because people praise you, adore you, and give you all the money they have. Stephen became very wealthy.

Carter told me that he heard Stephen Jeffreys stand before thousands of people in Africa and say, "Ladies and gentlemen, the world is at my feet to worship me."

He continued to preach his very simple sermons for some time, and they still were followed by remarkable healings. But the wealth began to affect him. In order to look more like a minister and less like a coal miner, he began to wear the attire of a Roman Catholic priest with vestments.

By the time I returned to England in 1936, however, Stephen was sick. I took a train to Wales to see him, because he had followed stories of my missionary tours with Carter through Tibet, Java, Siberia, and Russia. He wanted to meet me.

He had rheumatoid arthritis. I had to sit on the floor to look up into his face, and what a sweet face he did have! His head and neck were kinked over. His arms were twisted and his shoulders were twisted.

As tears ran down his face, he said, "I'm so sorry to have let this number one thing that I delivered people from come upon me."

I said, "I'm so glad to meet you. I have heard of all of your great revivals, and I have met people healed in those revivals in America, Australia, and different places. I just had to come see you."

He said, "Lester, it has been weeks since any preacher has come into this room. Not one pastor whom I gave a church to has come to see me."

"That is all right," I replied, "God sends in those who have a craving for the same kind of anointing that you used to have. I want you to know I will remember this day as one of the happiest in my life."

For several hours, I stayed and enjoyed the presence of a man who once operated under a great anointing and power, although he had lost it. Later, I asked my mentor, Howard Carter, how this could happen.

He said, "Lester, God will not permit His servants to have the gold or the glory" [that belongs to Him].

Out of possible ignorance, this boy from the mines of Wales accepted the glory that was lavished upon him by thousands of people. Stephen died soon after that, but he told me many things that have helped me.

Numerous churches had been started by Stephen out of revivals, but not one of the pastors from those churches ever came to see him in his last illness.

However, I learned from his example possibly one of the greatest lessons of my ministry. I try to pass it on to those young men who look to me for advice:

Stephen Jeffreys lost his power because no one had taught him not to touch God's gold or His glory.

A Different Brother, a Different Pitfall

George Jeffreys traveled with Stephen as his music director. Then he discovered that he was anointed with the same remarkable strength and power as his brother. However, there was a difference in their personalities. Stephen was exuberant, joyful, and a singing person, while George was sober, dark, and handsome.

George raised up Foursquare churches, while Stephen raised up dozens of Assemblies of God churches. There was no animosity or fighting — it just became two different highways for their lives.

George Jeffreys had a deep voice. He held meetings in the Royal Albert Hall in London, seating ten thousand or more people. It was jam packed, and hundreds could not be seated. It is likely that George became more popular than his brother for the simple reason he was so much more capable of organizing and handling funds. He handled the funds that came in through an organization, while Stephen ran the money into his own bank account.

I watched George Jeffreys in the Royal Albert Hall. His eyes were like fire. He could see that mighty congregation of more than ten thousand at one time. He knew their needs, and when he prayed, miracles happened — not as great as when his brother, Stephen, prayed possibly, but wonderful healings took place.

When someone in the royal family became sick, it was George Jeffreys whom they called, and they would pick him up in a limousine to come pray for the person who was sick. He was a very diplomatic man, however, and not a "name dropper" at all.

George Jeffreys also got off track when he read a book that caused him to believe that England was one of the lost tribes of Israel. When he taught this, at least half his pastors and churches left him. After a worldwide ministry, this erroneous teaching resulted in George going into seclusion.

The glory departed from George's life because he went after a cult and left the divine truth he had been taught from childhood. He went with the interpretation of men rather than staying with the teachings of the Bible.

I tell preachers all the time that there are three things they must watch: pride, material things and sex. God hates pride. There are outstanding men in the religious world in our country, but you cannot get to them for the simple reason they feel they are so important.

When you are successful, material gain will come to you. God wants you to be a channel. He does not want to build a dam and make you into a lake where nothing can go out but everything comes in. The Dead Sea is dead because it has no outlet.

Every minister of God must not only be a receiver, but he must be a giver. With greed or lust you can lose your relationship with God.

Most preachers are so innocent, they do not know that if they have a church with five hundred people, there may be a minimum of ten women who would give their souls to sleep with them just one night. They idolize their pastors. For them, to have sex with the pastor would be the greatest achievement of their whole lives.

A minister of the gospel must remember that he is a servant of a mighty God, and he is a servant of the people. He is not great. Only God is great. I have never met a minister who fell into adultery who *intended* to sin, or who set out to do this.

Joseph in the Old Testament was a type of the Lord Jesus Christ because he kept himself straight in all three of these areas.

When George Jeffreys died, there were only two lines in the newspaper: "George Jeffreys, an English evangelist, died on such-and-such a date" — a sad ending to great beginnings for a pair of brothers.

13

Carrie Judd Montgomery: A Bridge Builder (1858-1946)

I first met Carrie Judd Montgomery in 1934 at her Home of Peace in Oakland, California. I spoke at a couple of her Friday healing meetings in a downtown auditorium and prayed for the sick. Her husband had passed away some years before, and she ran her home for missionaries by herself.

She had people from all continents staying at her home at one time or another. A member of her family would make wooden crates in which the missionaries could pack their belongings for shipping overseas. He also would haul the crates down to the ships for the people and make sure they were shipped correctly to the right countries.

One morning when I stayed at her home as I passed through the San Francisco area headed out on the mission field, we were at prayer together.

She turned to me and said, "All the money God gives me today, I will give to you, because you are a missionary."

I thought, "Boy, I've got it made today."

However, all that was collected was $12, so I did not get much. But with the little money I did have, I bought some necessities for traveling and, when I started off on the boat, I still had $12. I suppose you could call them "Carrie Judd Montgomery" dollars.

She was more advanced in the knowledge and exercise of faith than many Christians in those days. Missionaries on furlough stayed with her to rest in a spiritual atmosphere, as well as missionaries en route overseas. Somehow, through faith, she was able to support this work, even after her husband, a successful businessman, died.

Many people have asked me how she was accepted among male ministers. As far as I can tell, there was no sense of competition with her, mostly because of the home that she kept. In the earlier days, however, women on the average were not very well-accepted. However, Carrie Judd was like a mother to young ministers. She was a true "mama" to those around her.

When I was there once, she said, "Come into my room, young man."

So I went into her private room, which was very large. It had its own fireplace and a sitting area, as well as her bed.

She said, "Now, you're going to take a journey of faith. I know Howard Carter. You had better be going in real faith, not hope. You get faith by studying the Word. You get in there and study that Word until something in you 'knows that you know' and that you do not just *hope* that you know."

I think she was trying to find out what was in me, what kind of backbone I had, and if I would quit and run home under difficult circumstances or go forward as God led.

Later, my wife and I and our children stayed with her on our way to The Philippines to build a new church in Manila. The children enjoyed the freedom and joy of her home. And we appreciated her so much.

She was everyone's friend in the ministry. Sometimes, she might have twenty different missionaries staying in her home at one time. And each one felt he, or she, had all of her attention. No one felt belittled or left out. Making everyone feel welcome is a special gift.

At that time, you could just give her whatever money you wanted to, or not give her anything, when you stayed at her home. It seldom made a difference to her anyway. She trusted God to meet her needs.

I usually tried to pay my own way there so that we would not be a liability to her.

Faith Through Adversity

Carrie Montgomery — a minister, teacher, writer, editor, director of a faith home, and a social worker — was reared in an Episcopal home in Buffalo, New York, one of eight children.

At the age of eleven she was born again and was later confirmed at the Episcopal Church. She knew then that she had a job to do for the Lord. However, two of her brothers and sisters died of tuberculosis, and Carrie herself was not well.

After a fall at Buffalo Normal School where she was attending, she became a complete invalid. She was forced to drop out of school and was not expected to live. However, through the ministry of a black woman, Mrs. Edward Mix, Carrie was healed.

Carrie wrote a book in 1880 called *The Prayer of Faith*, in which she shared her testimony of healing to encourage others to believe for healing.

A.B. Simpson, founder of the Christian and Missionary Alliance Church, developed a lifelong friendship with her through reading her book. Her miraculous healing also brought her into the leadership circle of the growing "faith-healing" movement of the late nineteenth century. She shared the platform with such notables as Charles Cullis,

W.E. Boardman, Maria Woodworth-Etter and Mrs. Michael Baxter of Bethshan, London.

Her literary career actually began at the age of fifteen when the Buffalo newspaper published a poem she had written. She later published other poems. She also wrote other books; however, her biggest literary output was *Triumphs of Faith*, a magazine she founded in 1881 and edited for sixty-five years.

Carrie Judd began to share her testimony.in public during the 1880s. She was a bridge builder between diverse religious groups. Carrie had religious ties with the Episcopal Church, the holiness and healing movements, the Christian Missionary Alliance, the Salvation Army, and the Pentecostal movement. She also was ordained as an evangelist with the Assemblies of God.

While she was still in Buffalo, she began a weekly meeting in her home. Soon "Faith Rest Cottage" was opened, a place where the sick could receive comfort, encouragement, prayer and teaching. The home was one of several established across the country in the late nineteenth century by people who believed in divine healing.

After ministering in the East during the 1880s, she moved to Oakland, in 1890. There, she met and married a wealthy businessman, George S. Montgomery, who owned property in an area near Oakland, later called Beulah Heights. Carrie and her husband established the "Home of Peace" in 1893 in a three-story Victorian house, which is still being used by the organization.

The Montgomerys established an orphanage from 1895 to 1908, which housed an average of fifty to a hundred children. In 1908, the Salvation Army took over its operation. They established Shalom Training School in 1894 to train missionary candidates.

Montgomery received the baptism of the Holy Spirit at the home of a friend in Chicago in 1908. At the same time, she was filled with a remarkable love for the Chinese. A number of Chinese understood her speaking in the Chinese tongue under the power of the Spirit of God.

A woman missionary of the Society of Friends who labored in China has told of being amazed to hear her singing in Chinese at a campmeeting in Beulah Park, Ohio, when they shared the same room. In the night they were both awake, and Sister Montgomery began to sing softly in tongues, and the missionary told her she was singing in a Chinese dialect to one of the tunes often heard in China. During the rest of the night she sang or talked Chinese in different dialects.

The missionary said to her: "You have not yet talked in Mandarin, which is my dialect."

Mrs. Montgomery said, "I will ask the Lord to let me speak in Mandarin."

The next morning at the meeting Mrs. Montgomery began to sing in Mandarin, which the missionary interpreted. Sometimes the most difficult Chinese songs were reproduced note by note. Twice the Lord gave Sister Montgomery the interpretation before the missionary could translate what she said. In each instance, the interpretation was verified by the missionary.

After her baptism in the Holy Spirit, she continued to maintain friendships with non-Pentecostals, such as A.B. Simpson and other Alliance leaders. Following a missionary trip around the world in 1909, Montgomery ministered in two of Simpson's services and spoke at four Christian and Missionary Alliance conventions.

She then published articles about the Pentecostal outpouring around the world. Her areas of emphasis were holiness and divine healing. Montgomery believed in speaking in tongues, but she felt that some people in the Pentecostal movement had put too much emphasis on it. She kept her emphasis on unity and love.

14

Peter Christopher Nelson: A Pilgrimage Through Darkness (1868-1942)

I first met P.C. Nelson in 1933 at a conference in Muskogee, Oklahoma. I had been asked to speak in the evening meeting. He taught in some of the day meetings.

One of the first things he told me after I finished speaking was, "Son, you need to come to my Bible school."

I even remember my message that day. It was on the Song of Solomon, and I had said the "sun" represented the Lord Jesus Christ, and the "moon" was the Church, because it had no light of its own. It is only a reflection of Jesus. He paid no attention to my sermon, which no doubt was very poor. I had only been preaching about two years.

It just happened that I had not heard about his Bible school. At that time it was located in Enid, Oklahoma.

I said, "I'd like to. Thank you for inviting me to your Bible school, but I don't think I'll be able to come. I am so very, very busy."

I kept hearing of him and then, in 1939 and 1940, I became better acquainted with P.C. Nelson.

He came by where I was staying and said, "My school needs food. Would you fill my carrier (a trailer on the back of his car) with food for the Bible school? My students are hungry."

With the help of the local church, we filled his car and his trailer with food. I was told that he did that all of the time in the Midwest — go to place after place and request food for his students. I had no idea then that he was Danish, because he spoke perfect English. As I got to know him, I found he was one of the most educated people I had ever met.

I helped fill his trailer on several occasions, and I am delighted that I had the opportunity. He even came to our church in South Bend with his trailer. I would sit and study him, and I could see there was something so much greater in what he was doing than in what many preachers were doing at the time.

By that time, I knew something about his life, and I do not think any of the early pioneers walked through as much sorrow and suffering as did P.C. Nelson. Truly, you could say the latter part of his life was much better than the former.

His father was disinherited by *his* father, who was a wealthy man, and imprisoned by the state, because he broke from the state church in Denmark. He become born again and was one of the first Baptists in that country.

Some people are only appreciated after their death. P.C. Nelson, a remarkable teacher and educator, was one of them. He left the imprint of his deep desire for the truth of the Word of God upon hundreds of young men so they would be prepared to meet the challenges of their generation.

Nelson, who became an evangelist, educator, and one of America's illustrious Pentecostal pioneers, was born in Ellitshoi, Denmark, January 28, 1868. He immigrated with his family to Iowa in 1872. Nelson's parents were honest and respectable. They were poor because they had been disinherited. P.C.'s father could not even bring his three oldest children with them.

America Was Not Kind to the Nelsons

A "friend" stole what money the Nelson's had, and left them almost penniless, stranded in Iowa with three children. Finally, they made their way to a little place called Cuppy's Grove and settled in a cave. Then the cave caught fire, and everything they had was burned. Then they were truly left destitute. Nelson wrote that, although they soon found another location, he was awakened many nights by wolves howling, prowling around, and clawing at the dirt that covered the other cave they had found. When they were able to build a twelve-by-sixteen foot cabin, they thought they were living in a palace.

Sometimes they had to wade through cold water to get to the cave, which only had a mud floor. In July, 1879, five years after coming to Iowa, where he thought America was going to be good to them, Nelson's father fell off a load of hay and died three days later. The three children were "farmed" out to neighbors to work and earn their food.

The family seemed to be plagued with calamities and tragedies. Within three months, Nelson's brother Nels died while a military engineer in the Civil Service of Denmark. His twelve-year-old brother Marinum died by drowning barely two years after his father's death. Frederick, Nelson's youngest brother, was institutionalized for mental and physical weakness, diagnosed as "incurable."

Nelson's older sister, Petrea, came to the United States from Denmark to be with the family. Within a year she began to show signs of insanity and within another year, she too was institutionalized.

At the time of his father's death, Nelson, eleven years old, went to live with a couple, who became his kind, Christian guardian parents for two years (1879-1880). In 1881, P.C. Nelson worked for Jacob Jacobson, father of a minister, who also showed much kindness and whose Christian example was a good influence. In 1882, P.C. worked on a farm but during the fall of that year, he had to stay home to take care of his mother who had suffered a broken arm and leg. She continued to suffer several such accidents.

During 1884, P.C. Nelson and his brother Thomas printed and sold visiting cards. In 1885 he began a four-year apprenticeship in the painting department of Cass and McArthur in Harlan, Iowa. During these four years, he attended school part time, and on June 1, 1888, he graduated in the Common School Course and received a diploma.

While in Harlan, P.C. Nelson became saved in meetings at the America Baptist Church and was baptized at the Harlan Baptist Church. That seems to have been a better year than usual for him, because it was also the year he met Myrtle Garmong, whom he later married.

Nelson's first "service" was at home with his mother, brothers, and sister. He was the only Christian in his family. After Nelson spoke until he cried and fell on his knees and prayed, his mother cried out to God for mercy.

Because of the persecution that followed this family meeting by some of the boys on the prairie where P.C. Nelson herded cattle, he denied the Lord and then felt he had committed the unpardonable sin. After nine years of wandering, Nelson was led back to the Lord by a pastor who assured him that he had *not* committed the final sin. That same night, he heard the Lord's call to preach.

In February, 1889, Nelson became a naturalized citizen of the United States. Later in the spring of 1889, he taught one term of school in Brown School House, thirteen miles southeast of Harlan. He read the Bible every morning and prayed in the school.

In August of that year, the church licensed Nelson to preach, after he had filled the pulpit at Harlan several times in the absence of the pastor. It was then that Nelson dedicated his life to go to the ends of the earth for the Lord. That fall, he began taking a course from Union Baptist

Theological Seminary in Morgan Park, Illinois. In 1890 Nelson left the seminary to enter Denison University in Granville, Ohio.

In the summers of 1891 and 1892, Nelson returned to his home in Harlan, where he spent the summers working at his trade and preaching as doors opened for him to do so. In September of 1892, he left for Denison University, this time accompanied by Miss Garmong. Baptized in water in the same baptistry at the same time, Nelson and Myrtle Garmong began to work for the Lord in the same church, she as organist and he as a member of the choir. They married in 1893.

In 1897, Nelson completed his bachelor's degree from Denison University where he specialized in ancient and modern languages, which he said was the most valuable part of his training. In 1899, accompanied by his wife and three small children, he moved to Rochester, New York, to study under Augustus H. Strong at Rochester Theological Seminary. It was Nelson's desire to read the Bible in its original languages that drove him to study so many languages. Nelson received his diploma in May, 1902.

After completing his studies, he entered the Baptist ministry as a pastor in Cedar Falls, Iowa. In 1904, Nelson went on the evangelistic field.

In 1920 Nelson, having served as a Baptist minister for thirty-one years, received the baptism in the Holy Spirit and embraced Pentecostalism. Because his congregation refused to accept his doctrines on faith healing and the baptism in the Holy Spirit, he resigned and spent seven years (1920-1927) in evangelistic ministry.

In October, 1920, Nelson's wife, broken in health but hungry for more of God, went to Carrie Judd Montgomery's home in Oakland, California, to spend time there. During this time P.C. was severely injured when he was struck by a car on a knee where he already had a carbunkle. His knee became infected and swollen, and blood poisoning began to develop. However, some friends came to pray for him and brought the message of faith and also of receiving the Holy Spirit. Nelson was healed through the prayer of a Pentecostal woman.

He was healed instantly, got up and dressed, and was waiting for the family when they came home that day. Some of them almost fainted to see him walking around. He also had terrible trouble with his eyesight. Later, a lady in Texas prayed for him, and God healed him of the eye problem.

His wife then returned in February, 1921, healed and baptized in the Holy Spirit. Nelson said she was a new woman. He made a commitment to make up for the thirty-one years in which he had preached a partial gospel. God gave him special faith to pray for the sick. Many people were healed of many problems and disease during the rest of his life.

Nelson visited some of F.F. Bosworth's meetings in Pittsburgh, seeing demonstrations of the power of God to save and to heal.

Southwestern Bible School in Enid, Oklahoma, which he founded in 1927, is now Southwestern Assemblies of God College, Waxahachie, Texas. The school was moved to Texas in 1943. He affiliated with the Assemblies of God. Nelson drew on years of experience as a missionary Baptist pastor and evangelist in his work for the General Council of the Assemblies of God, which began in 1925.

P.C. Nelson was concerned about worldliness and "anti-Pentecostal" attitudes in secular colleges and high schools. He felt that the Assemblies of God should look with favor upon Christian schools and that they were needed all across the country.

Nelson became well-known for his pulpit ministry, and he traveled widely to promote the Bible College.

15

Petrus Lewi Pethrus: The Great Organizer (1884-1974)

When Howard Carter and I were in China, we met a number of Swedish missionaries and preached in their missions. They wrote home about us, and a man named Lewi Pethrus, pastor of a very large Pentecostal church invited us to minister in Stockholm, Sweden.

Pethrus met us at the train station when we arrived in 1936. My memory is that he was not a very tall man physically, but he was very tall in the Kingdom of God. He was one of the best organizers I have ever known. As a young man, I learned a lot from him.

As Pethrus' church had began to grow after 1911, he found he needed a different and larger location. The one he found was adjacent to an ancient castle.

The government said, "Oh, no. You can't touch the castle."

But he said, "All we are going to do is have offices in the castle. We are going to build a large new auditorium next to it. After all, you don't want the castle to stand there and deteriorate. We'll take good care of it."

So the officials let him attach a four-thousand-seat auditorium. Very few people have the ability to merge the new with the very ancient and get the government to go along — but Lewi Pethrus did. Also, the church was built at the peak of the world-wide economic crash that began in

1929, in spite of protests from several of the church's wealthiest families.

When I first went into his castle offices, I was thrilled. I was still a young man who had never had an office. I had never seen anyone operate with secretaries and assistants. I watched very carefully how he did things. He was almost a "Solomon," in the way he exercised wisdom and did things the way they ought to be done.

He attracted the highest type of people and ran his church so well that he was a respected man in the country at that time, when he had been part of the "latter rain" of the Holy Spirit for more than thirty years.

He said to me during my first visit, "You know, I'm going to start my own newspaper, because secular newspapers don't print the truth."

And he did just that. In 1945, he founded the *Dagin*, which is still operating. At the time he was telling me this, I did not agree inwardly. I did not think a preacher needed a newspaper or that the people would want a paper published by a preacher. However, as it is still in operation, I must have been wrong on both counts!

Another wonderful thing about the Scandinavians of that era, which I noticed in the Pethrus home, was their appreciation of their mothers and their politeness toward them.

Pethrus had nine children living, one had been born stillborn. I loved his big family. We all sat at the table together, the mama and papa, the children, and whatever guests were there. In addition to thanking the Lord for the food, all of them would bow toward the mother and thank her for the good meal she had prepared.

Then, before they left the table, they would bow toward the mother again and say, "Your food was so delicious, Mother. Thank you."

I saw the same thing in Norway at Barratt's home, but I have never found the same courtesy and respect for mothers in any other country.

In a recent interview with one of his sons, I found that Pethrus was only eighteen when he was filled with the Spirit. Ingemar Pethrus told me his father was living in Oslo, Norway and involved in a small Baptist church at the time.

Ingemar said, "My father told many times of being sent one weekend on a little mission to one of the outlying cities where he spent the time witnessing. On Monday morning, the boat left to go back to Oslo at 3 A.M. He was standing on the deck watching the sun seeming to rise out of the ocean, when he began to worship and praise God. He found himself speaking words that he had never learned. That was in 1902, about five years before T.B. Barratt brought the message of Pentecost to Sweden."

From Baptist to Pentecostal

Baptized at age fifteen, Pethrus had grown up in the Baptist church. His destiny, however, was to become a Swedish pastor and international Pentecostal leader. A former herder of cattle and shoe factory employee, Pethrus heard God's call and responded wholeheartedly.

Following that initial experience, he served as an evangelist until 1904. In 1905 and 1906, he attended Bethel Seminary in Stockholm. He was elected pastor of the Baptist church in Lidkoping and served from 1906-1911. During those years, he began to read in the newspapers about the revival going on in Norway, so he went to Oslo in 1907 for teaching concerning the experience he had received on the boat traveling across a fjord early one morning. In 1911, he accepted the pastorate of Filadelphia Church in Stockholm.

T.B. Barratt was a great influence on Pethrus in his Spirit-filled walk with the Lord. His congregation, as well as other churches in Sweden, accepted the Pentecostal message. However, in 1913 the Swedish Baptist Convention expelled Pethrus and his entire congregation under the guise that they were practicing "open communion," which was against the church's doctrines. However, the real reason was because of their Pentecostal theology and liturgy.

Pethrus determined the priorities of the Swedish Pentecostal movement and represented it to the international movement. He tolerated no competition to his leadership, while he founded a rescue mission, a publishing house, a Bible school, a secondary school, a savings bank, and a worldwide radio network that reaches ninety countries and all the continents of the world. He instituted follow-up work, such as correspondence courses, for radio listeners in an effort to tie them into the church.

Pethrus also was a prolific author. His first book, *Jesus Kommer (Jesus Is Coming)*, was written in 1912 and is being translated into English by his son, Ingemar. This was followed by a ten-volume series on spiritual subjects, a five-volume series of memoirs, plus other books written after 1956. He also contributed many articles to periodicals.

Other ministry outreaches begun by Pethrus and motivated by his compassion for people, included high schools, relief agencies such as rehabilitation centers for drug addicts and alcoholics, small industries for patients, and special education opportunities.

Pethrus hosted the 1939 World Pentecostal Conference with twenty nations represented.

Again, we see in the life of another pioneer how God accomplishes His plans in what seems to us a roundabout way. In 1940, this Baptist-turned-Pentecostal was having some conflict in his church on account of one of the other pastors. So he came to the United States, serving as pastor in the Philadelphia Church in Chicago.

Pethrus was in the United States when the Assemblies of God in Brazil sent for him to settle some squabbles. As I mentioned previously, this denomination has no relationship with, and is not connected with, the Assemblies of God in the United States, Great Britain, Canada, or any other country.

At that time, the Swedish missionaries who followed Berg and Vingren had built large churches of three and four thousand people, funded mostly by Swedish Christians. Many of them had been sent by Pethrus's church. However, they would not turn their churches over to Brazilians. They would bring in another Swedish pastor, if one left.

Their movement was about to be deadlocked, when Pethrus went down there. He looked over the situation and here is what he suggested — which is what they did.

He said, "We are going to give every one of these big churches to the Brazilians. I want all of the missionaries to resign, give their churches to the best-qualified Brazilian, and get out of there.

"Then I want them to go to provinces in Brazil that do not already have works and start all over again. Run short-term Bible schools. Teach the Brazilians the Word of God and submission to God and one another so that they will not be wild and rebellious."

At that time, this policy of having natives run their own churches was not usual. Pethrus, however, was a born executive. He knew how to delegate responsibilities and get things done.

At one time, Pethrus sent fifty Swedish preachers to my church in South Bend. They called the group "the Swedish Men's Choir." Our people kept these men in their homes and fell in love with them, although most of them could not speak English. Pethrus knew how to pull people together and organize them. He became the greatest pastor in his country during his time.

After going to Brazil and straightening out the missionary situation, he heard clearly from the Lord to return to Sweden. He remained pastor at Filadelfia, Stockholm, until his retirement in 1958. He continued to be active in the Pentecostal movement until his death in 1974 at the age of ninety. He spent every winter of the last seven years of his life in Ventura, California, with his son Ingemar.

Lewi Pethrus was a very strong man. I have been in conferences where he stood up and adamantly opposed others. His spirit refused to lose, and he refused to go along with anything with which he did not agree. Until he decided to retire, he would never quit at anything.

Pethrus gave up his church because he thought it was time to retire, but there is no retirement in God. That is only man's idea. He was not allowed to speak in his own church when he returned there during his retirement years. I understand it nearly broke his heart. There is no telling what Pethrus could have done with his church if he had stayed in authority until he went to heaven.

Also, he would not put any of his children in a church position, although Ingemar and an older brother who preached in the United States for years could have been put in by Lewi as pastor of Fildelphia Church when he retired. However, he was so concerned that they be called of God and not be given a wrong advantage because of his position that he would not do it. I also believe that was a mistake.

Every Great Man Needs a Successor

Oftentimes, when God calls a person, he calls that person's family as well. Possibly, someone down through the years planted in Pethrus the idea that it is not good to promote your own family. However, to my mind, until you have produced a successor, you have not truly completed your life ministry.

In spite of possibly bending over backwards too much about his successor, Pethrus was a great man. Nobody had to tell Napoleon what to do. He instinctively knew what to do to win. Nobody had to tell Lewi Pethrus what to do. He instinctively knew. He knew how to handle the press. He knew how to publish books. He knew how to talk to kings, prime ministers, and congressmen. He could talk to anybody. People swarmed to hear him preach.

Ingemar Pethrus told me that he thought the most significant factor in his father's developing what came to be the largest church in his country was the fact that he could recognize the "gift" in someone else. He always was willing to give others an opportunity, except for bending over backwards where his children were concerned.

Pethrus also started the Christian Democratic Party (KES) in Sweden, the leaders of which include members of other denominations than Pentecostal. The party now has members in Parliament and in the Cabinet.

These men of greatness are our examples of selflessness, of not moving to improve their own well-being, but of plodding through trials and tribulations to strange and wonderful experiences in God. The next generation can rise up and call them blessed. We can thank God that the roots of our faith were founded by men of strength and men of wisdom, men who did not know what the word *quit* meant.

16

Victor Guy Plymire:
"Fenced With Iron"
(1881-1956)

I met Victor Plymire in Shanghai, China, in the 1930s. In those days, Shanghai probably was the most exciting city on earth. It was tough, unruly, and dangerous. It was the gambling center for the Orient. It was prosperous in the middle of the Great Depression, which extended world-wide, not just in the United States.

"Shanghaied" even became a coined word for being taken by force and made to work aboard a ship bound for another port, because this sort of thing happened so much in that Chinese port. This town on the coast of mainland China was the sort of place where, if you sat there long enough on the veranda of one of the main hotels, you would see everybody of any importance in the world.

When Howard Carter and I arrived there in 1935, we went first to what was called a "missionary rest home." In some of these great metropolises, usually one missionary would feel called of God to rent a very large place where those enroute to other missions could lay over and rest. These places were similar to Carrie Judd Montgomery's home in California.

Shanghai was the route to Inland China and to Tibet, by river and by train. It was the quickest way to Peking, now known as Beijing, the capital of China.

Soon after we arrived, I went out onto the porch while we were waiting for the evening meal to be served and sat down beside a man in a swing.

He said, "My name is Victor Plymire."

I said, "Oh, I've heard of you. You are a missionary from Tibet."

He said, "Yes," and as we talked further, he told me of how he had become involved in Pentecostalism.

"I was preaching in China," he said, "and God spoke to me in 1920 to go to Los Angeles. I left my wife and family and went. When I got off the boat, someone said, 'Have you heard there is a revival in this city?' When I said no, they took me to Azusa Street, where I received the Holy Ghost and began to speak in tongues.

As we continued to talk, and I asked questions, he said, "I was turned out of the Christian and Missionary Alliance Church because of Pentecostalism. Then I went back to China and Tibet as a faith missionary, not having any guaranteed support from anybody. Later, I joined the Assemblies of God and was supported through them at an allowance of $25 a month."

His wife and children went with him up and down those mountains preaching the gospel, trying to establish what we would call "house meetings." Someone would get saved and invite others into his home to learn about the Lord and serve Him.

He said, "My family knows what it means to ride the frigid trails of the top of the mountains connected to Mount Everest. They know what it means to go through the snow, to go over the rough rocks of the high Himalayas, to face hunger at times, and at others, to eat food that only the Tibetans enjoy."

I was so fascinated with this rugged person. He was about fifty years of age at that time and did he have stories to tell!

Carter and I had just returned from Tibet ourselves. We had gone the southern route, from Hong Kong through French Indo-China, which is now called Vietnam, on a boat. There we took a little French railway train back into Hunan Province, China. We had meetings all through that province and, from there, we began to move north and west for Tibet.

We had gone to the end of the road, to a place where there was no road and rented seventeen mules. One mule carried wooden boxes of rice, and another mule carried boxes of vegetables. As we traveled through the villages, the man we took along as a cook would buy anything he could find to eat and put in those boxes to cook for us in the evenings. Sometimes, there was not much to find.

However, in those high mountains we found "food" for our eyes. We saw beautiful butterflies, eight to ten inches in width. When they fluttered around your head and hands, you were more excited than you could ever imagine. There were many of them in those high mountains. Orchids grew wild on trees. We saw hundreds of them. They were so beautiful. You could reach up and get one or two to put in your lapel at any time.

Also, there were birds of many different colors. Those mountains seem to be a world apart. All the traffic was by muleback. No vehicular road had yet been made. And the mule road was just wide enough for two mules to pass. If you were not careful, your leg might get caught between the two mules passing one another and get smashed.

You not only had to remember to pull the leg up on the passing side, but you had to remember that below you, on the outside, was a long drop to the bottom. Each mule tried to steal as much of the road for itself as possible, so the ones on the inside would be trying to push the outside mule over the side of the mountain or into the mountain on the inside.

Because of having been there, I understood his stories about evangelizing in Tibet. This was a man of remarkable strength, because he dealt with mules all of the time. He had to load and unload them every day. Plymire told me how God had spoken to him and called him to go and live in Tibet and preach the everlasting Gospel to the Tibetan people. He had learned to speak their language very well.

He told stories of people more than of great revivals and large numbers, individuals who came to know Christ and stayed with their convictions no matter what it cost. What it cost both his wives (his first wife died in Tibet) and his children to move about like this from village to village and town to town, no one will ever know.

We sat in that swing until someone said, "Dinner time. Would you please come to dinner?"

I said, "If I can sit by this man, I'll do that," because I did not want to leave him.

Howard and I spent some time in Shangai that trip, preaching in the city and staying in the rest home, so I was able to spend some time with Plymire.

China at that time was in the throes of an immense disintegration. Mao Tse-tung was coming from the far west out of Russia with guns and ammunition for the Communist revolution. He was attempting to set up a new Bolshevic empire equal to Russia's. Joseph Stalin was supplying everything Mao needed.

We had discovered also as soon as we reached the northern parts of China that the Japanese already were there. We did not know this was a forewarning that, in a few short years, Japan would also embroil the United States in World War II.

Japan had occupied the capital of China, all of Manchuria, as well as all of Korea. Every time we went to church, there were Japanese militiamen standing in the back in battle uniform with guns held in their hands. They never moved a muscle during the whole service, but stood there like statues.

We had an interesting visit in Shanghai that year. Plymire and others had come out of the interior where war was raging. Chiang Kai-shek was battling to get his armies out of China and over to the island of Formosa, now called Taiwan, at the time.

From Pennsylvania to China

Plymire was born on January 10, 1881, to Christian parents in Loganville, Pennsylvania.

When he was sixteen, Plymire consecrated his life to God at a street meeting and began attending the Christian and Missionary Alliance Church (CMA).

God called him to full-time Christian service from his work with an electrical construction company. He sold his equipment and began to attend the Missionary Training Institute in Nyack, New York. Later, he was ordained by the CMA Church. He pioneered several churches in the United States before being accepted as a missionary in northwest China on the border of Tibet in 1908.

There were many struggles and hardships in Tibet, but Plymire trusted God and continued to work. Only after sixteen years was he able to baptize his first convert. What patience this man had!

In 1919, he married Grace Harkless, daughter of a mainline denominational missionary family in China. She and a baby died of smallpox in 1927. A year later, Plymire married Ruth Weidman, a missionary to China. Plymire and his new wife continued to minister in Tibet until 1949 when China, which controlled Tibet, closed to missions.

Back in the United States, he pastored churches in Ohio and Missouri until his death.

I cannot tell Plymire's story any better than Charles E. Greenaway, missionary to West Africa and founder and president of Continental Bible College in Brussels, Belgium, did. He wrote:

> If Victor Plymire had lived in David's day, there is no doubt in my mind that he would have been included in this select group (David's "mighty men of valor," whom he called "fenced with iron" in 2 Samuel 23:6,7). These men were not born great men, voted great men, chosen great men, but were mighty because of their actions on the field of battle . . . and so was Victor Plymire.
>
> To get to his first destination, he traveled three months up the Han River on a filthy riverboat, infested with cockroaches and rats. . . . He slept with animals, ate spoiled meat, lived on raw vegetables (and ate dirty food mixed with hair and debris).
>
> He braved the elements. He loved them (the Tibetan people). He sewed up their sword wounds, washed their ulcers, pulled their teeth. He faced death many times, making his way to monastery after monastery. He felt the brazen powers of hell as he watched them worship their gods in dimly lit temples. He witnessed their sacrifices of gold and silver to these gods . . . .
>
> Plymire, it seems, was in perpetual motion . . . fighting snowstorms . . . or almost dying of thirst on the plains. He hunted for and found the monastery where (the Dalai, or Grand Lama, a man thought to be the present reincarnation of) Buddha was living. He was allowed to see him. Plymire told him about Christ. (He was the first white man to visit there and the first person to tell them about Jesus.)[1]

Plymire learned to eat Tibetan food the hard way. The bandit who taught him the language gave him a dish of spoiled meat one day. Plymire could not eat it, so the man

---

[1] Greenaway, Charles E. "Fenced With Iron, Part I," December, 1986, p. 27 and "Fenced With Iron, Part II," *The Evangelist*, January, 1987, p. 21,22.

set it before him the next day — and the next. Finally, crying out to God for help, Plymire was able to eat the meat. This hard lesson of never refusing what is set before you probably saved his life in Tibet many times. Refusing the food would have been a great insult.

One of the secrets of Plymire's success was that people back in the states prayed for him. On one occasion when Plymire and two devoted followers were about to be executed, a prayer warrior in Olympia, Washington, was awakened by the Holy Spirit to pray for him.

After seeing a vision of a group of men with swords surrounding three men in a tent, she obeyed. She recognized one of them as Victor Plymire, who had spoken in her church. She prayed fervently, and Plymire's life was spared in the final moments before the proposed execution.

The woman who prayed later wrote to Plymire describing the vision the Holy Spirit had shown her. He said that if a photographer had been there, he could not have taken a more accurate picture.

Plymire's son, David, is still a missionary to the Chinese.

17

Charles Sydney Price:
A Prince Among Preachers
(1887-1947)

My first introduction to Dr. Charles S. Price was when I was between eighteen and nineteen years old, and someone gave me a small magazine, one-fourth the size of a regular magazine, with approximately a hundred pages. It was called *Golden Grain*.

I wrote to the address on the magazine and asked for a copy of every issue they had published. I received a package of magazines about two feet high.

That winter I was in Green Forest, Arkansas, raising up a church I had sponsored through a crusade. I was setting the church in order and getting a pastor for it. Not much was going on in the hills of the Ozarks at that time, so I spent any extra time going through each of those magazines. It was somewhat like taking a university course in theology. Price was very well-educated and had experienced remarkable events in several denominations.

Another native of Britain who deeply affected the Pentecostal movement in the United States and worldwide, he was trained in law at Oxford and then emigrated to Canada. On a visit to Spokane, Washington, he was converted at a Free Methodist mission. A pastor there convinced him to enter the ministry.

He had an opportunity to become involved in the Azusa Street outpouring, but another minister convinced him that was not of God. Instead, he influenced Price to steep himself in what became known as "modernism," the school of higher criticism that began in Germany mixed with what was called "the social gospel."

He ministered in the Methodist Episcopal Church, then moved over to the Congregational denomination, pastoring a church in Alaska. During World War I, he was a public speaker for war bonds, becoming very popular in the San Francisco area. He accepted a pastorate in Lodi, California, after the war.

Here the Lord brought the Pentecostal experience to his attention for the second time. Members of his church began to attend Aimee Semple McPherson's meetings in nearby San Jose. He related later that he went to the meetings, intending to discredit Mrs. McPherson.

Instead, he heard a powerful message that "punctured" his modernistic theology "like a sieve." The power of the Holy Spirit began to fall in his church. When denominational officials interfered, he started an independent church, Lodi Bethel Temple.

In 1922, Dr. Price began to itinerate as an evangelist. He began to stir the world in a very unique manner. After reading that stack of his magazines, I wanted to see him very much. On my first trip west trying to find Howard Carter, I was three months behind him. But I found Stanley Frodsham.

Stanley said, "Would you like to hear a truly great preacher?"

I said, "Oh, yes! I would."

Frodsham said Dr. Charles S. Price had a giant tent set up in Pomona, which was nearby. He also told me that he knew Price personally, both having been born in England, and he would have me not only introduced to Dr. Price but seated on the platform.

I was simply elated. It was more than I could even imagine at my young age, to be sitting on the platform behind this great man. The tent was packed for the afternoon rally, with many people outside sitting in their cars. Some others milled around looking for a place to sit during the sermon.

He preached like a man from another world. He could talk about even a flower and make you see it. The congregation was fascinated, and so was I, at his descriptions that brought Bible characters to life. After he prayed for the sick, he came over to us, hugged us, shook our hands, and thanked us for coming to hear him.

This was in the 1930s, and he was not a young man at this time. You could see the maturity in his face, not just age. When I told him I was on my way around the world, he laid his hands on me without my asking for it. He asked the Lord to give me a special anointing for the nations of the world. I had never heard a prayer before for being anointed to minister to the nations of the world in evangelism.

When he was through praying over me, I thanked him and then confessed, "Sir, I have preached a lot of your sermons."

He said, "Praise God! I'm sure glad they are worth that much."

I said, "Oh, sir, your sermons are the richest field I have ever been able to find in which to get material. I spent the whole winter in a rather small town in Arkansas. Every day and late at night, often until midnight, I read what you had to say.

"Very often, new sermons sprang up within me, even sermons that I illustrated for the people. I became very close to you in the spirit through your magazines, and I want to thank you for giving out the truth in such a remarkable and beautiful manner."

And he was so gracious, saying, "Well, I'm so glad my sermons are usable, and I'm so glad that God is going to use them with value through you as you travel."

So I continued on my way around the world, and Price continued in his mighty tent meetings, auditorium meetings and sometimes church meetings. In later years, when I preached in Belleville, Illinois, he was there. Thousands of people came to know the Lord in the Missouri and Illinois sides of the Mississippi River because of the preaching of Dr. Charles Price. He was a man of great intellect, great force, and great faith.

In Granite City, the church where he preached ended up with one of the largest congregations in the area, mostly from the converts made during Price's meeting.

He Was a "Regimenter"

So we rejoiced in the ministry of a man who was born in London, who was a resident of Canada, and who now worked for the Lord in the United States. Dr. Price was a "regimenter." For example, when you came to his tent to receive healing, you had to hear at least three sermons, indicating the three sermons you had heard on the prayer card. He would not permit anyone to be prayed for until they had heard him preach at least three times.

At first I did not understand why he did this, but later I realized he was building faith inside of them for healing. He preached at least two hours every service.

He handed out cards and each person who wanted to be healed was given a number. Before he got up to speak, he had created a healing line. He would say, for example, tonight we will take numbers 216 to 275. That may not sound like many out of a crowd of ten thousand. However, in addition to the healings of the people with prayer cards, many people in his audiences received healing without hands being laid on them.

He did not just lay hands on people, he got them healed. He would stay with them until the healing came through. It might take an hour for him to pray for just a few people because he prayed in depth for deliverance. People were set free by the mighty power of God.

Dr. Charles Price commanded deep respect as one of the greatest teachers, pastors, and evangelists of the early Pentecostal movement. He ministered extensively in the northwest area of the United States and Canada. Before his death, he also ministered in Sweden, Norway, England, Egypt, Palestine, Turkey, Syria, Lebanon, Italy, and other parts of Europe.

18

Raymond Theodore Richey:
A True Pioneer
(1893-1968)

I first met Raymond T. Richey, the first of all these pioneers whom I knew, when I was almost ten years old. He came to Laurel, Mississippi, where we lived at that time and held a meeting at the Courthouse, the largest auditorium in the city. At that early age, I witnessed my first healing revival and never forgot it.

He was a master of the stage, although he was a man of small stature and had no deep or commanding voice. However, he was a master of words. Unlike Dr. Charles Price, his sermons were short, but people were miraculously healed in his meetings. When he said, "Come to Jesus," people literally ran down the aisles.

I saw people get so excited about giving to God that they literally ran down the aisles and threw their money on the platform until it was covered. Richey did not "beg" for anything, but when the miracles began to take place, an atmosphere of praise would come upon the people, and they would give to the servant of the Lord.

We had seen people healed in our church one by one, but we had never seen people healed in such numbers in one service. The first introduction into such a ministry is exceedingly exciting, especially when you have been taught that the New Testament is true and the things that are reported in it were real. My first exposure to Richey's healing services was like seeing the New Testament literally come to life.

Raymond T. Richey was a loveable person. I hardly remember anyone who truly disliked him. He knew how to get along with people, particularly people in leadership such as governors and mayors. He spoke with such sincerity, telling of his own healings, that people felt a sympathy and a love for him.

He accepted an invitation to come to my father's house for dinner after the meeting in Laurel. You cannot imagine how honored we felt with this man of God at our table — talking, praising God, rejoicing in the Lord, and loving us. We thought it was the greatest day of all our lives. I sat very near him, and joy seemed to flow from him.

One of my older sisters, Anna, was not well at that time, and he asked, "May I pray for her?"

Anna was healed immediately when he laid hands on her, and as a result, she developed a strong relationship with the Lord. Our home was a brighter place after the visit of Raymond T. Richey. I lost touch with him then until after I began to preach.

In 1930, when I was about seventeen years old, I conducted a meeting in Tulsa, where Richey had just completed a mighty revival. The healings in his meetings were so numerous that there were great trucks loaded down with wheelchairs, walking canes, crutches and other types of medical appliances removed from people when they were healed.

Once again, as a young minister, I was as touched and influenced by his ministry as I had been as a youngster.

Raymond T. Richey, born on September 4, 1893, in Illinois, became a renowned healing evangelist. He grew up in a home where his parents accepted divine healing. In fact, his mother was healed from tuberculosis, and his father, Eli, claimed healing from cancer.

When Raymond was young, the family moved to John Alexander Dowie's city, Zion, in order to live in a faith-charged atmosphere. Eli Richey eventually became mayor of Zion City, where he also had a prosperous business in real estate.

As a young boy, Raymond Richey's eyesight began to fail because of a serious injury. However, when he was eighteen, Richey attended a healing meeting conducted by Archibald P. Collins in Fort Worth, Texas. It was at this meeting that his eyes were healed and he surrendered his life to Christ.

Five years later, in January, 1916, his father accepted a pastorate in Houston, Texas. At this point, Raymond surrendered to the call of God on his life and became assistant pastor to his father at Gospel Tabernacle.

Unlike Lewi Pethrus, Eli Richey used his family in the ministry, with four of his eight children working as a team as the congregation began to grow.

After the United States entered World War I in 1917, Richey established the United Prayer and Workers' League for the distribution of literature. He also set up a tabernacle on Washington Street in Houston near Camp Logan with funds provided almost miraculously. Thousands of soldiers attended, and at least hundreds were converted to Christ.

As Richey ministered to the dying soldiers during World War I and the influenza pandemic which followed, he contracted tuberculosis. Before he received a miraculous healing for the tuberculosis, it is said of Richey:

> Elijah-like, Richey prayed that he might die. God graciously reminded him that he had been miraculously healed of an eye disease not long after his conversion, that his mother had been delivered from this same dreaded tuberculosis, and that the church back home was having special prayer for him . . . .

Richey took his Bible and read Psalm 103:3: **Who forgiveth all thine iniquities; who healeth all thy diseases.**

Creeping slowly from his bed and staggering weakly back and forth across the room with his Bible raised overhead, Richey murmured, 'I praise You, Lord. I know that You are healing me.' Each time he repeated these words his voice grew louder, until he was shouting at the top of his lungs. In that hour he was made "every whit whole." It was only normal to expect such a man to have an exceptional divine healing ministry.[1]

Raymond T. Richey was a pioneer evangelist in the Full Gospel movement. Gospel Tabernacle grew so fast that in 1920, the old building had to be replaced. More than fourteen hundred people were attending, and in the next five years, the facilities had to be enlarged twice more.

In the meantime, Raymond began his evangelistic crusades and held successful crusade after crusade across the United States, always returning to Houston. Finally, in 1927, Evangelistic Temple was built on Capitol Avenue. The greatest ministries of the day came to Houston for crusades.

Fire and flood threatened this work in the early 1930s; however, immediately after this building burned in 1932, it was rebuilt. In 1935, flood waters totally filled the basement but rose no higher, so that major disaster was averted.

The building was not the only thing about the Richey's ministry that was tried and tested. In the 1920s, some attempted to pull them down by raising questions about Raymond's marriage to Eloise Mae Richey. His wife's previous marriage had been annulled, so not even divorce was in question. The minister who had married them, A.P. Collins, also came in for criticism.

---

[1]Assemblies of God Archives, 1445 Boonville Avenue, Springfield, Missouri 65802.

However, both the physical and spiritual building programs undertaken by the Richeys for God withstood the attacks and flourished.

During World War II, Richey had a great tent fabricated in red, white and blue. He put that tent outside of large military posts, and servicemen were saved by the hundreds. Richey knew how to communicate with the average soldier as well as with generals and colonels.

Richey Never Stopped Moving With God

As World War II came to a close, Richey took the tent overseas to Seoul, Korea, to serve the Korean and U.S. military personnel. This was possibly the beginning of the great revival that swept South Korea, although Dr. Yonggi Cho, being much younger than Richey, probably never knew him.

I preached in South Korea in Presbyterian churches in 1935 or 1936, about the time Dr. Cho was born. Those churches, as far as I know, were the original "cell group" Christians there. They also pioneered "prayer mountains." The entire church would go up on a mountain and yell out to God as loud as they could. The most spiritual churches in the Presbyterian denomination that I have found were those in Korea.

Missionaries from there also went to Chile and possibly to Peru, because when I traveled there, I met some of those Korean preachers whom I had met in Korea.

Richey was part of the first great wave of twentieth-century revival, but when new waves of revival came, he was not one of those who held back and said, "What I have is good enough."

He flung himself into every revival from the first wave in this century right on up until his death. In fact, he moved out as a leader in the healing revival. He was a friend to Gordon Lindsay, Oral Roberts, F.F. Bosworth, and others.

When his father died in 1945, Richey returned to Houston to pastor Evangelistic Temple. Southern Bible School which his father had started, had been consolidated in 1943 with Guy Shield's Shield of Faith Bible School and P.C. Nelson's Southwestern Bible School.

In the 1950s, Richey continued his crusade ministry with trips to Central and South America in 1951 and trips to Germany, Switzerland, Japan, and Korea in 1957-1958. A new co-pastor was called to take over the leadership of Evangelistic Temple. In August, 1966, two years before Raymond Richey's death, the congregations of Evangelistic Temple and Central Assembly of God merged, maintaining the name Evangelistic Temple.

Richey had a pioneering spirit, and he was not afraid to move into new territory, places the devil thought he owned.

In the last great revival on Planet Earth, we need men like Richey, with deep courage, great faith and tender hearts. We need men like Richey who are able to rise up unselfishly and bless multitudes. We need people who will fling themselves wholeheartedly into every new move. We do not just need the "sons of the prophets" today. We need the prophets themselves!

We need people with pioneering spirits. Raymond T. Richey was the kind of minister men and women ought to be today. We need people who will do as he did. Richey was not hesitant to start over when it became necessary to reaffirm his foundation, and he would move into areas where no ground had been broken before him.

Above all, Richey was a man who cared for other people. He always asked about my parents and about my brothers and sisters. He became a lifelong friend until, like the Old Testament patriarchs, he lived out the full measure of his days. He touched my life in such a way that his memory will never fade.

19

James and Alice
Salter

James Salter:
"Wise Counselor"
of the Congo
(1890-1972)

I met James Salter, mostly because he was Smith
Wigglesworth's son-in-law. The relationship between Salter
and Wigglesworth was very beautiful to see. If you spent
much time with the two of them together, you could see
that Smith loved Jimmy like a son. And James Salter loved
his father-in-law so much that he sacrificed time with his
wife and put aside his own needs in order for her to look
after her father in his last days.

Salter had met Alice Wigglesworth after he had spent
about five years evangelizing in the Belgian Congo. She
and other missionary recruits returned to Africa with him
in 1920, and he married her soon after.

I sat in his meetings and listened to him teach. Almost
every sentence was a new thought, as concisely put as if he
had worked on it for a long time. Salter was a very friendly
person and one of God's leaders. His testimony was
always, "God is a good God."

Also, in private conversation, he was able to talk about
anything you wanted to talk about. He never had the

notoriety that his father-in-law had, and I do not think he ever sought it. However, I do not believe he ever was really in Wigglesworth's "shadow."

In other words, marrying Alice Wigglesworth did not cause him to be overlooked or overshadowed. I believe it made him greater. I believe it blessed him and gave him encouragement. He was a very gentle, non-assertive person. I almost felt he was too easily satisfied, that if he got a small piece of pie, he would feel it was enough.

Salter was a man who spoke well, preached well, and loved others. His task in the Congo was to help the Congolese build an economy, to teach the people trades as well as get them saved and filled with the Spirit. Then he trained those called by God to be native pastors.

The Congo Evangelistic Mission, founded by Salter and W.F.P. Burton in 1919, built one of the greatest missionary outreaches in the world. Through Wigglesworth, a lot of funds were supplied in later years to carry on the mission.

Salter became so beloved by the people that he was given the Congolese name, *Inabanza*, which means "wise counselor."

Another man of short stature, Salter was as at ease with immense crowds as with small groups. Like his father-in-law, he had devotions — a "word" from the Book — at every meal, and ministered as if he were speaking to the entire Body of Christ.

Traveling in the Congo was by no means a luxurious experience, although it was not mountainous nor filled with the other hazards of Tibet. However, in Tibet, they only killed people — in the Congo, they ate them.

The paths through the jungle were so overgrown with grass at times that the missionaries were not able to follow them very well. Also, there were lions, wild elephants, and all sorts of dangerous bugs. On one occasion, Salter woke up to find that he had slept all night with a snake. He knew because the snake left his skin behind.

Thorns pierced them as they cycled and walked along the snake-like paths. Wild nettles also stung them almost unbearably. The heat quickly left them with sodden clothing and squelching boots. When the rivers were in flood and the streams high, at times they would have to remove their clothing in order to keep them somewhat dry as they waded into the water. They had to assist their porters, who otherwise might have been swept off their feet and drowned.

Also, they faced witch doctors and those who believed in them. Salter wrote later that no method was too "devilish" for the witch doctors. He said spiritualism was very common, and mediums were kept busy and considered very important people.

He wrote, "Their messages are always given in an unnatural ecstasy and whilst under control of the 'spirit.' I have seen one of these mediums give the closest imitation to a person under the power of the Holy Ghost, even to the stammering lips."

In an article he wrote thirty-two years after his first trip to the Congo, Salter said:

... I never shall forget our first night on the Congo River. We looked for a place to camp, and we came across some fires smouldering; there were large pots on the fires, and inside there were human bodies cooking; human bones were on the ground. We had settled on the site of a cannibal feast.... (The team had to stop there. It was too dark to go further. However, they did not sleep!)

As we cycled through the villages, they would come running after us, calling to each other, "Come along, there is some white meat here on bicycles." But there are no cannibals in this place now. There are twenty-eight churches there; they have put up their own buildings, and they have their own pastors.[1]

---

[1]Salter, James, "When Pentecost Came to the Congo."

Over the years, he wrote many articles to various Pentecostal periodicals telling of the dead being raised, lepers being made whole, and all manner of diseases and infirmities being healed.

Africans Had a Hunger for God

Salter told in his trips back home to Britain and in meetings elsewhere that the people in the Congo were so hungry for more of God that they would not even eat or sleep, but kept the missionaries talking sometimes all day and all night. Many received the baptism of the Holy Spirit before they ever read about it in the Bible. The baptism came in response to their hearts' cries, "We are hungry."

However, those first converts did not come easily. Salter faced many a situation that looked impossible in those early days.

Salter believed that "God is the God of the people who are at their wit's end, who are right up against it with their backs to the wall, and He delights to come to our help when we need Him most . . . . All He asks for is that simplicity of faith which will take Him at His Word."

He wrote:

> They poisoned our water and our food; they tried shooting poisoned arrows at us, and then bullets. It was easier to dodge the bullets than the arrows. . . . We were among people whose language we had to learn word by word . . . . In those first months, I tramped from place to place, preaching the gospel, until my whole body was soaked with malaria.[2]

Three times Salter was supernaturally healed of blackwater fever for which there was no known cure. Twice more, his life was despaired of as he lay near death from other causes. It was through the supernatural healings of

---

[2]*The Pentecostal Evangel*, Feb. 14, 1948, p. 2, from a talk given by Salter at Central Bible Institute.

Salter and of many natives that the people began to believe in Jesus. Once they heard the stories from the Bible, however, they became hungry for the gospel.

Salter served on the executive council of the Assemblies of God of Great Britain and Ireland and was chairman of their conference. In later years, after he left to live in Great Britain, he returned to the Congo regularly, sometimes for lengthy visits.

Perhaps the greatest sacrifice of his life for the good of the Kingdom was allowing his wife, Alice, to travel with her father and spend much time looking after him, while he went back to Africa alone. He died in England at the age of eighty-two, unlike many of the missionaries who had remained in Africa, or had gone there later.

His associate, Brother Burton, also was an outstanding man of the times, a very brilliant person. In fact, I think possibly that doctrinally as well as in preaching ability, he was the leader of that entire large group of British missionaries and some Canadians who joined them. Burton was stronger than Salter in a lot of ways, and he had a consuming appetite for greatness. The two men worked together as a team like twins.

They had great projects. They taught farming and other skills to the natives. They taught pastors and raised up teachers for Bible schools. They were all first-class workers and loved and cared for one another. They almost were a world unto themselves.

However, after World War II, when the white governments were overthrown and the native peoples took over running the various African countries, what the missionaries had done for the people somehow was forgotten. Many times they were killed by their own workers, people whom they had loved, trained, fed, and clothed.

I think something James Salter wrote once is good advice for all of us: "(Our life in the Congo) is not all bright, but dark patches can serve to make the other parts seem brighter."

20

Douglas R. Scott:
Apostle to France
(1900-1967)

I know that God has a sense of humor, because He created Douglas Scott. He was one of the funniest men I ever met. Without much education or Bible training, Scott felt led of God to go to France.

No human being has ever chopped up the French language as badly as Douglas Scott, but he was so innocent in it that the people roared with laughter. He would say things he did not mean to say simply by mispronouncing the language. But when he laid hands on people, they were healed. Scott was able to move among the upper echelons of society in France because of the healing miracles that took place in his ministry.

When I visited Scott in France, he kept me in the mayor's home.

One day, one of the mayors where Scott visited said to me, "Young man, what year were you born?"

I said, "Nineteen hundred and thirteen."

He marched out of the room and came back with a bottle of wine marked "1913."

He said, "I have wine in my cellar downstairs from every year of this century. Whoever eats at my house must give me his birthdate, and I bring him wine, laid down to age in the year he was born."

He opened the wine and all of us had a little sip of it. Douglas Scott was not a wine drinker, but he would sip a third of a teaspoon full, laugh victoriously, and start telling stories of healing. The mayor of the city became fascinated with the little Englishman.

Sometimes I think Scott should have been in the circus. He wore suspenders, and he would take his coat off in public, which no upper-class Frenchman would do at that time. In the midst of elegant people, he would be the only man present with his coat off, even when he was preaching from the pulpit.

If he had been one of the higher-class Englishmen, I do not think they would have accepted him as easily. But he was of the workingman's class. Everyone loves a "court jester," and he was one.

He would take hold of his suspenders and say, "I want to tell you about God," and the people would roar with laughter.

If Scott wanted to emphasize a point, he would pull one of his suspenders out, turn it loose, and "pop" it. Then he would pull the other one out and pop it. The French people would scream with laughter.

He had a "baby" face, and the mouth of a movie actor — very elastic and expressive. The French people loved to watch the way his moved his mouth around trying to pronounce French words. They would correct him from the audience when he made a big mistake.

He would say, "Thank you very much," and keep going. It did not bother him at all to be corrected.

France is a nation famous for humanism since the late 1700s and also for the individuality of the people. They do not like to be the same as other people. As for really liking other nationalities, they usually do not. They do not like the

Germans, and they do not like the British. But they liked Douglas Scott.

Scott started a large church in Rouen, France, a great industrial city. I was there when he had over a thousand people in his church. Then he began a church in Paris. He began churches in Marseille, Nice, and Monte Carlo, all along the French Riviera.

Scott's wife was sweet, but as different from him as chalk from cheese! All she could do was smile for her husband and agree with everything he said. She would read the Bible to him in French and try to get him to repeat it so he would speak it right.

At that time, the wealthy people of Europe came to Nice for their vacations. Scott's church was full of these people, and they loved him. Monte Carlo was the gambling capitol of the whole world, yet the people there loved him.

The French had no ability to raise up these churches, but Scott would go and "beat the devil to pieces." Then he would bring people into the church, baptize them in water, and get them full of the Holy Ghost.

Scott was influenced in his Christian growth by Howard Carter, Donald Gee, and Smith Wigglesworth in England, so he organized the churches he started in France as the Assemblies of God of France.

God took Scott, a man who belonged in a factory, and made him one of the greatest spiritual leaders I have found anywhere in the world. Scott never said what he was going to do. He just did it. He never stayed anywhere long enough to own a home. He went from city to city in France and raised up churches full of the Holy Ghost, God's blessing, and His anointing.

Scott left his mark on France for a whole generation, and he endeared himself to the French people. Scott loved people and the French people loved him in spite of all the funny things he did. Because he was full of the Word of God, he led the French people in the right way, and a French revival was brought about.

A "Court Jester" for God

Scott was born into a religious family in Essex, England, and as a young boy, he attended a Congregational Church.

At twenty-five years of age, Scott was born again when he heard a Polish Pentecostal student preach about the cross of Jesus. A few months later, he was baptized in the Holy Spirit as hands were laid on him by George Jeffreys. He also was supernaturally healed of a speech impediment.

Scott became involved in street meetings and in door-to-door evangelism when he dedicated himself wholly to the Lord's service. He went to Le Havre, France, in 1927 to learn the language planning to go as a missionary to French Equatorial Africa. However, Scott began preaching in his limited French at a mission in another French town. Healings followed the preaching of the Word.

Being urged to return and minister in Le Havre, he sought confirmation from the Lord and received it through a word of prophecy. In 1929, Scott married a Frenchwoman, Clarice Weston. The next year, the Scotts moved to Le Havre where Scott played a key role in establishing the Pentecostal movement in France.

Scott held revivals in Normandy, southern Belgium, western Switzerland, and southeast France. The Scotts spent the war years in the Congo and evangelized in French North Africa from 1952-1956.

Scott was recognized as a man of the Spirit who always sought the Lord's guidance before he acted. He was direct in his preaching, made the Scriptures come alive, had a great sense of humor, and was driven by compassion.

He was God's man, he knew it, and he was a blessing. He was a little younger than most of the other pioneers, but he was a pioneer in France. He left his mark there.

I do not suppose he ever met a person he did not like. He was the biggest hugger and kisser you ever saw. He just loved humanity. And he recognized that he was almost a layman and that it was God's power that was raising up those churches.

Others of the pioneers preached in France, but they only passed through. Scott was a man who did not pass by. He raised up churches and young men to pastor them. You might say that he almost built a denomination on his own.

I would sincerely agree with those who call Douglas Scott an apostle to France.

21

Lillian Hunt Trasher: The Great Mother of the Nile (1887-1961)

This book would not be complete without a word about another remarkable female Pentecostal pioneer: the irrepressible Lillian Trasher. She was a pioneer in quite a different way than any of the others.

I wrote the first full-length book of her life, which was published in 1951. Loren Maclay of Glasgow, Scotland, wrote the foreword to the book. Maclay had visited Trasher's orphanage personally and wrote these words: Lillian Trasher "has brought into being one of the largest and best-equipped orphanages for children and needy ones in all the East."

In 1950, I traveled by train from Cairo to Assiut, Egypt, to visit Lillian and her orphanage. I arrived about midnight extremely weary from the journey.

Lillian had already retired for the night, but in the guest room I found a pot of hot chocolate and a handwritten note, "Hi, Les! Have a good night's rest. Lil."

I thought, "What on earth is this woman like? What kind of a person am I going to meet tomorrow morning?"

The following day I met a large, jovial American lady who radiated happiness through a broad smile and keen sense of humor. She carried no serious look of profound care, but looked as if feeding a thousand children each day was just a way of life.

Possibly she thought I was doing enough worrying for both of us, because I could not see how she could feed so many. She was a woman of incredible faith. Her happy spirit constantly spread laughter and sunshine throughout the entire orphanage.

Lillian Trasher began her world-famous orphanage in 1911 with one diseased baby. Since then more than six thousand have called the orphanage "home." More than five hundred children and widows live now on the twelve-acre campus.

The orphanage is a large compound resembling an estate with gates and at least thirteen buildings, arranged for different age groups to live in, including a special section for widows. In that part of the world, widows used to be left to die.

Once I asked Lillian, "What is the one thing, greater than any other, that you are trying to do in Egypt?"

She looked at me with a twinkle in her eye and said, "I have been trying to live in such a way as to pass something tangible on to a new generation. I would like to pass on a disposition of Christian character. I try to transmit to the children that if they can trust God, everything will be all right.

"I do my best to teach them to have faith in God so they will be able to face life with a heart of trust. I try to pass on to them a power — a power of prayer and a power with their fellowmen — that they may teach others how to find the way. I would like to show these children the greatness and grandness of sacrifice. I would like them to know that if I had not come to Egypt they might have died of neglect."

She wanted them to know that, not for her sake, but in order that they might also understand how important it is for Christians to live that kind of life.

In Islamic territory, the Lillian Trasher Orphanage is a lighthouse beaming the love of Jesus Christ to the nation of Egypt through the lives of thousands who have grown up there. Most of the children called her "Mama Lillian" because she was the only mother they ever knew.

I continue to support the orphanage with hundreds of dollars a month, even though Lillian has gone on to be with the Lord.

Lillian Trasher knew how to handle people whether they were Americans, Britishers, or Egyptians. She was very bold in her approach. When she could not get any money from America to feed her children, she went to the wealthy Egyptian people.

If she needed something, she would go knock on the door of a rich man who would say, "Come in and have some food with us."

She would say, "Not until I get money, I won't. My children are hungry. Give me the money to feed my children. I want to buy a thousand pounds of rice."

People gave her money, because she literally demanded it.

After they gave her the money, she would say, "Now I will eat with you."

When the presidents and prime ministers held banquets, Lillian Trasher was always invited. As she was escorted into these formal events, she would come in spreading sunshine, and the whole court would applaud.

The master of ceremonies would introduce her this way: "Ladies and gentlemen, the great Lillian Trasher, the Nile mother."

She was more than six feet tall and weighed more than two hundred pounds, and she would enter those formal rooms with all the dignity of a queen, dressed beautifully. She never dressed poor.

Sometimes she would be the only person to receive applause out of all of the dignitaries present at the festivities. Although Lillian Trasher lived with the poor in a little room on campus, she also knew what it meant to go neck and neck and face to face with the millionaires of Egypt.

When I first saw Lillian's operation in Egypt, I asked, "Has anyone ever written a story about you?"

When she said, "No," I promised to write a book about her.

I was on my way around the world, but when I got back to America, a stack of her monthly letters and all kinds of papers were there to greet me. From these materials, I wrote her story, *Lillian Trasher, Nile Mother*.

Lillian was not a preacher, although at one time in her life, she pastored a successful Pentecostal church in the United States. She was a smart businesswoman and clever.

She had to be to feed her charges. Food was cooked twenty-four hours a day to keep all of the children and widows fed.

She was a woman of such courage that it did not matter who you were. When it came time for her to get money to feed her children, you had to cough it up, because she was going to have it. I like that kind of person. They are very exciting to me. From the king on down, when she came in the door angry, they knew to get their pocketbooks ready.

I met a man on her campus when I was there the first time who became a very good friend. That was Philip Crouch, uncle of Paul Crouch, founder of Trinity Broadcasting Network. Phil and his wife, Hazel, began to work with "Mamma" Lillian in 1948, and he helped make an award-winning documentary on Lillian's life in 1955. He is now manager of the TBN television station in Dallas.

Phil wrote that she was never bothered by her size but used it to great advantage in crowds or on the streets in Egypt. People would recognize her because of her size and offer gifts for her orphanage. He called her "a legend in her own time," and I agree.[1]

An Unlikely Missionary

Lillian was an unlikely "missionary," who reached Egypt via Ohio, the Carolinas, and Africa. Born in Florida to a successful Roman Catholic businessman, in her late teens she got hold of a Bible of her own and became converted at a friend's Bible study group.

She wrote once that she was "appalled" to realize that she grew up in "so-called Christian America" without knowing anything about the greatest book ever written. Once she saw one at a friend's house in Atlanta, however, she did not rest until she had a Bible of her own.

She attended God's Bible School in Cincinnati for one term, then left to work in a North Carolina orphanage. Then she attended Altamont Bible School in South Carolina, where she received the baptism in the Holy Spirit.

Although the church she pastored was very successful, she left to accompany an evangelist on tour, then returned to the orphanage in North Carolina. During the tour, she became engaged and later proved that she meant it when she talked of giving up everything for God.

The young man's heart was not in missions, so she broke off the engagement only ten days before the scheduled wedding in 1910. Then she traveled to Africa in

---

[1]Crouch, Philip. "Why They Called Her the Greatest Woman in Egypt," *Assembly of God Heritage*, Winter, 1984-85, pp. 7,8.

the face of her family's strong objections. However, a sister did go with her and was a great help during the times of severe persecution which Lillian went through before finding her true calling.

She was ordained with the Church of God in Cleveland, Tennessee, in 1912, and by 1916, she had fifty children in a home in Assiut, which is more than two hundred miles south of Cairo, Egypt. She joined the Assemblies of God in 1919.

As part of her role as "mama," she delivered hundreds of babies, which if they were girls, usually were promptly named "Lillian." She is buried on the orphanage site in Egypt. She was one of the most unusual women I have ever known and a pioneer of a different kind.

Lillian was a true pioneer of spiritual strength. Full of the Holy Spirit, she was a woman who demonstrated Christianity in its rarest form. No doubt at this very moment she is enjoying the riches of heaven because she gave so much away while she was on this earth.

Her life is a testimony that the only way to do great things for God is to do small things first.

Alfred George Ward:
A Man Who Knew
His Weapons
(1881-1960)

In A.G. Ward and his son, I saw the first combination of a dynamic father and son ministry. I have personally spoken in conferences where both of them also were speakers. It was very delightful to see the admiration the father had for the son and the son had for his father.

In fact, in spite of an illustrious career, Alfred George Ward may be known best for his role as father of C.M. Ward, the now-retired speaker on the long-running radio program, Revivaltime. Faith and miracles dominated the lives of both father and son.

A.G. Ward was born October 11, 1881, in a log house located on his grandfather's farm near Prescott, Ontario, Canada. His father was an alcoholic who died two months after his birth. Although he was the youngest, A.G. outlived two brothers and a sister.

Because of the struggle his mother faced in raising four little children without any financial means, she died when A.G. was only thirteen. He already had told his mother that someday he would be a preacher, although he later said, "nothing seemed more unlikely." He worked hard to get through high school.

Before his mother's death, Ward attended revival meetings in the Methodist Church, although his family was Episcopalian. He did not have a born-again experience at that time because the altar counselor did not explain the necessity of repenting for his sins.

After high school, he was appointed home missionary for the Methodist Church of Canada. This made him "a pioneer circuit rider on the great western frontier under the shadows of the Canadian Rockies on the Calgary-Edmonton trail."[1]

Even on his second circuit term, he called himself a "young preacher without a real experience," and would tell often of preaching himself under conviction as he held meetings in homes. There were no church buildings and sometimes not even a school in which to meet.

During his second tour of duty for the Methodist Church, he was on the Blindman Valley circuit in what later became the province of Alberta in western Canada. At the most northern point of his circuit, he found a group of people who believed in divine healing. Originally from Kansas, they had moved to Alberta to homestead land.

When he accepted Christ, he found that the deep, mysterious longing that had been in his heart for years was realized. Instead of going on to seminary as was required in the Methodist Church, he decided to attend a holiness Bible school. He realized that, even in those days, much unbelief was already being taught in mainline seminaries.

Not many years later, Ward joined the Christian and Missionary Alliance (CMA) denomination. He became a friend and acquaintance of its founder, Dr. A.B. Simpson, who had been a major figure in the holiness movement of the nineteenth century. Simpson was a strong believer in divine healing.

Of the baptism of the Holy Spirit, Ward said that it was his "greatest education." It occurred as he traveled across

---

[1]Ward, C.M. *Intimate Glimpses of My Father's Life*, Assemblies of God, Springfield, Missouri, 1955, p. 10.

Canada for the CMA as a field evangelist. He heard over and over about the mighty outpouring of Azusa Street. After he received the baptism, Ward said that the Bible became a new book to him.

Over the years, he spoke in new tongues, some of them known languages which he had *not* known: German, Indian, Swedish, and Polish. Ward wrote that a life of prayer and a life of praise such as he had not known before opened up to him.[2]

Multitudes were delivered and healed and mighty miracles were wrought under Ward's ministry by the laying on of hands. From a preacher who preached without being saved himself, Ward progressed into a man of God who truly knew that his weapons were spiritual.

Ward learned to take authority over death as well as sickness, when he faced a persistent battle with the healing of his own daughter, Ruth, as a ten-year-old with a tubercular knee. After having the elders of his church pray for her, the Wards carried her around for weeks praying for healing.

Then one day, he said the Lord told him, "I don't want you to ask Me again to heal your daughter. I want you to begin today to *thank* me for her healing."[3]

In a very little while after that, healing began to manifest in the knee, and she was completely healed. This experience was of great benefit in the influenza pandemic when the parents and all three children were struck down. Two of the Ward children were near death's door, but faith triumphed, and all were healed.

In 1919, A.G. Ward was ordained with the Assemblies of God. From 1919-1926, he served as an itinerant evangelist.

---

[2]Ward, C.M., *I Saw the Spirit Move in These Meetings*, Assemblies of God, Springfield, Missouri, 1956, pp. 25,26.

[3]*Intimate Glimpses*, p. 28.

From 1926-1928, he pastored Central Assemblies of God in Springfield. From 1930-1938, Ward was actively involved and served the Pentecostal Assemblies of Canada first as secretary and then as secretary-treasurer.

When Dr. C.M. Ward left Canada to become an instructor at North Central Bible College in Minneapolis, Minnesota, A.G. Ward, also joined the staff. The father and son were almost inseparable.

A.G. Ward retired in 1950. So rich was the spiritual legacy of his parents that Dr. C.M. Ward wrote, "I would rather have been born into such a house than be given the honor of sitting in the White House. God is real to my life. He is the very breath I breathe."[4]

---

[4] *Intimate Glimpses*, p. 4.

23

Smith Wigglesworth: Apostle of Faith (1859-1947)

Dr. Howard Carter, with whom I traveled for many years and who sent people all over the world to minister, told me of Smith Wigglesworth. In my travels around the world, I heard other reports about Wigglesworth until I wanted to see him more than any other prominent minister of the day. There was an eagerness inside of me to hear and see Smith Wigglesworth.

After I had been with Carter through Australia, the Orient and all through Europe, we returned to England for a national conference. Carter was chairman of the conference which was held in Cardiff, Wales, and he asked me to speak in the evening because I was an evangelist. He had asked Smith Wigglesworth to speak in the afternoon because he was a teacher.

The first week I was in Great Britain, my dream came true. I was teamed up with the man I had wanted most to meet. He did some teaching that afternoon and prayed for the sick. We sat on the platform together and smiled at each other.

"I've surely heard a lot about you, Brother Wigglesworth," I told him.

And I was very pleased when he replied, "Yeah, and I've heard a lot about you. I've been reading your articles for two years. Man, some of those stories about casting out devils! I like that. And your trip up to Tibet and back — I'm just glad you're not afraid."

So we kind of made a friendship there. Wigglesworth heard me preach that night. Now, remember, I was still a very young man, and not extremely experienced although I had been preaching since I was seventeen. I preached the best I could, and I did give a successful altar call. When I was through and turned around on the platform, there was Smith Wigglesworth looking at me.

He put his hand on my shoulder and said, "Son, you need to come see me."

In school, I had been called into the office, and I knew what it meant to face the principal and work on a problem. My first thought when Wigglesworth said I needed to see him was that I was being called to the principal's office.

I said, "Yes, sir, when can I come?"

He said, "Anytime. I live in Bradford. Here's my address and telephone number."

I said, "How often can I come? Do I need to let you know I am coming?"

He said, "You can come as often as you want to. These days I am home, so you don't have to let me know. Just knock on my front door, and I will open it. I'll always be glad to have you."

The next day, they had what we call "dinner on the grounds" in the southern United States. They had long, long tables loaded with good food. In the center was a roasted pig, which had been basted with oil and other good things as it was roasting.

However, they made a big mistake — they asked Smith Wigglesworth to say grace. He walked over to that table, a big, healthy man, raised one hand to heaven, and said,

"Almighty God, if you can now bless that which you have cursed, bless this foul pig to their bodies."

I looked around and thought, "Dear Lord, and we have visitors here!"

But those Welshmen tried to hide from him. They were the ones who had brought the pig and roasted it.

I went over to him and said, "Are you having a piece of pork today?"

He said, "I never touch the stinking stuff," so I had an introduction to the way he would say anything he thought ought to be said anytime and anywhere. He had no fear of man whatsoever.

Within a week after that conference I was on my way to Bradford. When I showed up at Wigglesworth's house, I had "gone native." I was a real Britisher with a bowler hat, similar to the one you saw Charlie Chaplin wear in his early movies, a black jacket, striped trousers, and a dark blue raincoat that came just above my knees. I wore beautiful pointed black shoes and had an umbrella under one arm and a newspaper under the other. I carried my briefcase in one hand.

My Personal Time With Wigglesworth

They did not have electric doorbells, but I grabbed the knocker and hit the door with it, then stepped back three or four steps.

When Wigglesworth opened the door, I said, "Here I am, Brother Wigglesworth."

He did not respond, just glared at me, and said, "Hoots under your'm?"

That meant, in his British accent, "What is under your arm?"

I said, "I have an umbrella under this one and the morning paper under this one."

He said, "Throw it away. You can't come in here with it. I don't permit those lies into my house. Hitler and Mussolini will soon be in hell where they belong. In my house, there's only truth, and that paper's full of lies — so leave it outside."

Hastily thrusting the paper into the bushes beside the door, I said, "Yes, sir; yes, sir; yes, sir!"

When I came back out, someone had taken it, so I lost my paper altogether that day.

He then looked me over and said, "Cm'n." We went into the living room where he had a coal fire on, and it was very cozy. I thought I had come to talk, but he read to me a half hour from the Bible.

Then he said, "It's time to pray," and he prayed for another half hour. He laid hands on me and prayed, "God, bless him! God, bless him!" My body was becoming weary. I was glad when he got through!

Basically Smith Wigglesworth was a "Bible man," who enjoyed reading his Bible to visitors and equally enjoyed praying long prayers over the reading. So he read to me from the Bible for another half hour, then said, "Let's pray again."

Inwardly, I said, "Lord, what did I get into here? This man will wear anybody out."

Your body can become weary after hours of this, but it seemed to bring a tremendous refreshing to Wigglesworth. Finally, he got up from his knees and began to tell beautiful stories of how God had healed this disease and that condition. I sat there weeping, absolutely overwhelmed.

At noon, his daughter, Alice Salter, called us to lunch. She had prepared Yorkshire pudding, roast beef with that delicious gravy the British put on it, and peas. We had a delightful time of fellowship.

When we got through, he put his napkin on the table and said, "Come back again."

Then he walked away. His daughter explained that he had gone to get some rest.

Before I had gone a block from his house, I said to myself, "You know, I got something there. I'm different. I got something. I received a blessing. I received an anointing. Something good happened to me in that place. I'll come back again."

I received life in that house. Both father and daughter had life. About ten days later, I went back. Oh, yes, I had on my little dark-blue raincoat, and I had my umbrella and my bowler hat — but I did not have a newspaper!

I continued to go to Wigglesworth's house about every ten days for two years. I continued to listen to him read the Word and pray, and I heard personally of the mighty miracles God had done for him around the world.

My faith began to mount up strong in the presence of this man. We became good friends. When he had a convention, he would ask me to speak also. We would meet in other conferences in addition. Once a year, Wigglesworth held a convention of his own in Preston, which is in the northern part of England.

He invited me to speak while I was in England, along with his son-in-law, Jimmy Salter. It was so interesting to watch him chair a meeting. He did it just as he pleased. You never knew from one minute to the next what was going to happen.

He just let the Holy Spirit direct the meeting and tell him what to do. He did at least tell me I was to speak in the evening, so I did not have to be concerned all day long about when I was to speak. He was very unconventional, a man of the Holy Spirit with a heart full of faith in God.

In the two years that we had fellowship, however, I never met another visitor at his house.

Nor did I ever hear him say, "So-and-so was here yesterday, or will be here tomorrow."

Never once did he mention anyone visiting him. At almost eighty, he was kind of a forgotten man, amazed that a young man would just come and sit at the feet of an old man. I was having the time of my life, but I think he was too. He got lonely there by himself, just him and his daughter. When I had to leave England, he became very emotional. I suppose he felt another lonely period coming.

It was only after his death that people began to say, "He was a great man," although they had talked of what people thought of as his eccentric ministry and of the great miracles that occurred in his meetings. He had shaken nations overseas more than his home country.

He had made a tremendous amount of money in his overseas meetings, particularly on the Continent. But he lived very thriftily, because he funneled the majority of his offerings into missions as fast as he got it. He particularly supported Salter's efforts in the Congo. He never cared about money for himself. He lived by faith.

I wanted what this man had. His bluntness intrigued me, and his depth of sweetness was like a well of water springing up. It was so delicious that I would come and drink again and again and again. However, Wigglesworth was abrupt. He did not believe in wasting words.

One day, I asked him, "Brother Wigglesworth, how is it you look the same every time I come? How do you feel?"

He bellowed at me like a bull and said, "I don't ever ask Smith Wigglesworth how he feels!"

I asked, "How do you get up in the morning?"

He said, "I jump out of bed! I dance before the Lord for at least ten to twelve minutes — high-speed dancing. I jump up and down and run around my room telling God how great He is, how wonderful He is, how glad I am to be associated with Him and to be His child."

After this, he would take a cold shower, read the Bible for an hour, pray for an hour, then open his mail to see what God would have him do that day. He was an extremely remarkable man, totally sold out to God.

A Prophecy of Hope in the Middle of War

In 1939, World War II broke out as Germany invaded Poland. I had preached all over the continent, and I knew it was coming. Everyone in Britain knew it was coming. I had preached in three hundred and nineteen cities in the two years before this, in Great Britain and Europe, especially in France.

I had even preached in Germany with Hitler's Gestapo men sitting in every one of the meetings, although they were still allowing outside ministers to come in and preach. However, I knew when I went to England in 1937 that it would not be long before full-scale war broke out again.

War clouds hovered over Europe and Great Britain during most of the late thirties. Prime Minister Neville Chamberlain made such a miserable failure at handling Hitler, returning from a meeting with him waving a piece of paper in his hand and proclaiming "Peace in our time!" When, of course, everything Hitler had agreed to was a deception and lies.

Sir Winston Churchill had been barking at Chamberlain's feet for months and months about his handling of Hitler, so of course, when war broke out,

Chamberlain had to resign. Churchill then became prime minister.

Hitler's armies moved through Poland, Belgium, Holland, and into France. The French had thought the Maginot Line would hold the Germans, but Hitler went down through Holland and came around the "invincible" line of defense. France fell in six days. I have not only lived through spiritual upheavals caused by wave on wave of the Holy Spirit in this century, but through all of the natural upheavals caused by all of the wars of this century.

I cannot describe what it was like, living in such exciting, yet such unsettling, times — particularly those two years that I was in England. The British were very apprehensive, even frightened, those who were not pacifists backing Chamberlain with their heads in the sand.

Also, Churchill visited the United States frequently, pleading with President Roosevelt to get involved. He thought that Hitler would not dare to attack Britain if he knew the United States would back up England — and he may have been right. At any rate, Roosevelt did not declare war until he had to, when Japan attacked Pearl Harbor on December 7, 1941. So when I was there, I was among Britons, who felt very lonely and exposed in their island empire, not very well-prepared for war.

One morning someone knocked on my door at the Bible school where I was staying in London, and I opened it to find a big policeman, more than six-feet tall, standing there with a paper in his hand.

He said, "I'm looking for Lester Sumrall."

I answered, "I'm Lester Sumrall."

And he handed me the paper, saying, "His Majesty has sent this notice to you that you have ten days to leave the country. This is now a war zone, and Hitler is getting himself in position across the (English) Channel to hit us conveniently. As you are a visitor here, you will need to leave."

If I had not left then, before open hostilities broke out, there was no telling how long it would have been before I could have left the country safely. I began to visit friends I had made there to tell them goodbye.

I went to Smith Wigglesworth's home to tell him goodbye. It was a sad visit, because I knew I probably would not see him again in this world.

He had blessed me in so many ways. He had discussed the Word of God with me in many wonderful sessions, so that I was always eager to get to his house. And he seemed eager for me to come. At that time, I was in my mid-twenties, and he was eighty in 1939. I suppose not many young men were interested in spending time sitting at the feet of an old man, no matter what his life had been.

I said, "Brother Wigglesworth, I am on a special mission today. I have orders from your government to leave the country. It is nothing I have done. It is what Hitler is doing."

Explaining that I only had so many days to leave the country because of the expectation of an imminent Nazi attack, I told him I planned to go back to the States and then on to other countries to continue preaching the gospel.

I said, "The fellowship with you has been very rare. Only a person like Howard Carter or Donald Gee has blessed me equal to the blessing I have received from you, and I humbly thank the Lord and thank you for giving me so much of your time.

"I thank you for letting me hear you talk to God in prayer and hear you read the Word of God and see how it comes alive within you. I am grateful, but now I will have to leave."

Wigglesworth stood up, and tears began to flow down his face. He looked like a "Philadelphia lawyer" or a "Boston banker," not a hair out of place and, as always, groomed so perfectly and beautifully.

He stood as straight as a general and said, "I want to bless you."

He laid his hand on me and pulled me close to him, and I let my head go in closer to him. Tears flowed from his eyes and ran down his face and dropped off onto my forehead and ran down my face.

As he cried, he said, "Oh, God, let all of the faith that is within my heart be in his heart. Let the knowledge of God that resides in me also reside in him. Let all the gifts of the Spirit that function in my ministry function in his life."

I just stood there weeping, and he stood there praying and weeping, holding me in his embrace. I felt the holy anointing of the Most High God as it flowed from him into me.

As he broke the embrace, he said, "You will be blessed and faith will reside within you, and you will do unusual things."

Then he stopped a moment, opened his eyes, and said, "I wish to tell you something," and his eyes looked as Elijah's must have when he saw the chariots of fire coming. I said, "Yes?"

He exclaimed, "I see it. I see it."

I asked, "What do you see?"

Shutting his eyes again, he said, "I see the greatest revival in the history of mankind coming to Planet Earth, maybe as never before. And I see the dead raised. I see every form of disease healed. I see whole hospitals emptied with no one there. Even the doctors are running down the streets shouting."

He told me that there would be untold numbers of uncountable multitudes that would be saved. No man will say "so many, so many," because nobody will be able to count those who come to Jesus. No disease will be able to stand before God's people.

It will be a worldwide situation, not local, he said, a worldwide thrust of God's power and God's anointing upon mankind.

Then he opened his eyes and looked at me and said, "I will not see it, but you shall see it. The Lord says that I must go on to my reward, but that you will see the mighty works that He will do upon the earth in the last days."

In spite of being sad at leaving him, his words excited me. The idea that I would get to see this revival was almost overwhelming. And in the last decade or so, I believe we have seen this revival begin to sweep the earth. We have seen amazing moves of God in Africa. We have seen enormous congregations raised up all over the world.

Recently, I was in China and met with the underground church. I was told there are at least forty-five million Full-Gospel Christians in China. I discovered a depth of prayer and integrity there that I have not felt anywhere else in the world. There is something so intense in those Chinese Christians that you have to join in with them.

When they weep, you weep. You cannot help it. They told me of at least a hundred people who have been raised from the dead in recent years. They told of blind eyes opened, people walking out of wheel chairs, and of a mighty revival moving through China. So I believe we are seeing Wigglesworth's prophecy begin to be fulfilled. We are seeing the first stages of it.

My feeling is that this revival will not last a long time, but that it will come upon young men and women who are not well-known nor greatly appreciated. Suddenly, their names will be everywhere because of the mighty move of God in their ministries.

In the last couple of years, perhaps twenty-five different pastors in twenty-five different places have said to me that the Lord has told them this mighty worldwide revival will begin in their locations.

I have just smiled and thought, "Well, I don't care where it starts, just so I get to be in on it."

The Exciting World of Smith Wigglesworth

When Smith Wigglesworth was born in Yorkshire, England, and came to live and eventually minister on Planet Earth, evangelism was largely centered in Great Britain and was led by British ministers. Beginning with the second quarter of the nineteenth century, Britain had begun to take the gospel to the ends of the earth beginning with Inland China.

There had been few missions efforts since the days of the Early Church. Evanglization from about the fourth century on had been to gain converts for the Roman Catholic Church, and after the Reformation, evangelization still continued to be mostly among believers and centered on doctrines.

In the eighteenth century, many British ministers — Methodists, Baptists, Presbyterians — had spread out across the vast continent of the United States working with the Native Americans. But no major worldwide effort of taking the gospel to the ends of the earth (Mark 16:15-18) had taken place until about 1830.

Then organized missionary efforts and organizations began to be formed in Great Britain. The British Christians sent Hudson Taylor, Adoniram Judson, William Cary, and others to China. David Livingston went into Africa, and William Booth founded the Salvation Army.

Smith Wigglesworth knew these pioneers who were British intimately. He knew the pioneers of Pentecostalism. He often ministered with the Jeffreys, Donald Gee, Howard Carter, T.B. Barratt of Norway, Stanley Frodsham, and most of the others I have mentioned.

Of a truth, he was born in very favorable times, surrounded by unusual men who blessed and inspired one another. And, like many other great men, he came from a humble beginning. Much of this has been told in detail in Frodsham's books and in books by others about Wigglesworth.

He was hardly known beyond his hometown of Bradford until he was forty-eight years old when he received the Pentecostal experience at Sunderland under the ministry of Episcopal Vicar Alexander Boddy and his wife. Until this time, Wigglesworth was a plumber and assisted his wife, Polly, in a mission.

She did the preaching, and he greeted people at the door, passed out books, and counseled at the altar.

From the time Wigglesworth was six years old, he helped support his family, first by pulling turnips then by working in a factory with his brother and his father. Because he was deprived of an education, he never learned to read until he was an adult. In fact, his wife taught him to read. In later years, he said that he never read anything but the Bible.

Wigglesworth was converted at eight years of age at a Wesleyan Methodist Church. At ten, he changed to the Church of England and was confirmed. He was sixteen when he went to the Salvation Army. At twenty he moved to Liverpool to work. He won hundreds to Christ, particularly the poor children who lived near the docks. He fed them from his salary and preached Jesus to them.

At twenty-three, Wigglesworth returned to Bradford, where he made his home for the remaining days of his life. There, he opened his own plumbing business and met the young lady who was to become his wife.

Wigglesworth received healing from a ruptured appendix. As a result, he said that God gave him great faith to pray for people suffering with appendicitis. He began his healing ministry before he was baptized in the Spirit. He usually concluded his sermons by praying for the sick.

Polly Wigglesworth died before her husband began to be well-known and to preach extensively in other countries. In his later years, he became one of the best-known evangelists in the Pentecostal movement.

He was accused of being "rough" with people, but he was never accused of being weak in faith.

Of course, I heard about him long before I ever met him.

In Sidney, Australia, a pastor asked me, "Have you ever met Smith Wigglesworth?"

I said, "Not yet. I'm on my way. I'm going to find him somewhere. I have heard of some of the miraculous things that happen in his unique ministry."

The pastor said, "He was here in my city recently, and did we ever have a time! I took him to one of the fanciest restaurants to have lunch on Sunday. When we came into the restaurant, someone took his coat and hung it up for him. He looked around like an eagle. Only wealthy people ate in this restaurant. Instead of sitting down, he took a fork and began to hit the side of his glass with it. Bing! Bing! Bing! Bing! Everybody stopped eating.

"Here was Wigglesworth, a handsome-looking man, beating his water glass. Then he raised his hand and said,

'Ladies and gentlemen, I have noticed since arriving here that none of you prayed over your food. You resemble a bunch of hogs to me. You just jump in and eat without giving thanks to the One Who provided it for you. Bow your heads, and I'll pray for you.'"

The pastor told me, "I could have crawled under the table very easily and gotten out of the way so people wouldn't see me. Wigglesworth raised his hands and prayed for those people. Before we left the restaurant however, two families came over and got saved. Then I was ashamed of myself for not being as strong as Wigglesworth."

Wigglesworth's ministry centered on salvation, healing, and the baptism of the Holy Spirit. He was strong in character and created his own atmosphere wherever he went.

After receiving the baptism of the Holy Spirit, the Lord spoke to Wigglesworth to prepare a banquet for the poor, the lame, and the blind. He secured tickets and hired two people to go throughout the city and find the afflicted, the tormented, and the crippled and bring them to a supper he would provide at the mission.

He often said the sight of those suppers was beyond description, and that this was the happiest time of his life. The mighty healings that took place during those times increased Wigglesworth's faith.

During the 1920s, he came to America on several evangelistic tours. The first time I heard any specific details of his ministry was in San Francisco before starting around the world with Howard Carter.

I was preaching at the Glad Tidings Tabernacle, which seated more than three thousand people.

People said to me, "Have you met Smith Wigglesworth?"

I said, "No, not yet," and they told me he had been there in the same tabernacle where I was preaching. They told me of a cancer patient brought to the healing service.

Wigglesworth went down the line, saying, "What'sup?" British-ese for "What is wrong with you?"

When he got to this man lying on a bed wearing only a little hospital gown that tied in the back, Wigglesworth asked the doctor with the man, "What'sup?"

The doctor explained that his patient was dying of cancer.

Wigglesworth asked, "Where is it?" and the doctor replied, "In his stomach."

The evangelist promptly balled up his fist and hit the man in the stomach so hard the man appeared to die. His hands fell off the bed, and the doctor began to scream, "He's dead! He's dead!"

He looked up at Wigglesworth and said, "You've killed him! The family will sue you!"

Wigglesworth calmly looked at the doctor and said, "E's 'ealed." He talked with a Cockney accent, not pronouncing his "h's."

He did not stop but kept on walking down the line praying. About ten minutes later, the man came down the line behind Wigglesworth on the platform. He had stood up, moved the doctor to one side, and was walking around in that funny little hospital gown with his backside hanging out before more than three thousand people!

He did not have one thought for his appearance, however. He had his up hands over his head and was screaming, "I'm healed! I'm healed!"

Even the doctor had developed faith. He was right behind the sick bed yelling, "He's healed! He's healed!"

The man caught up with Wigglesworth and said, "I have no pain. I feel wonderful inside. I have energy I have not had for I don't know how long," but Wigglesworth never even turned around to look at him.

He just said, "Well, thank God for it," and went on praying for people. It was no big surprise to Wigglesworth. He already knew the man was healed.

That was the first time I had heard a detailed story of Wigglesworth's ministry, although I had heard about him since I was a small boy.

After hearing this story, I thought, "Say! Someday I want to meet him."

Then I went to New Zealand and Australia and heard more stories, including the incident in the restaurant, which only increased my desire to meet this man. When I met him I was not disappointed. He was just what I expected him to be from all that I had heard about him from the people of the nations I had visited, where he had conducted meetings.

Some ministers found Wigglesworth *too* strong in faith, and that frightened them. Also, he was strong in rebuking them for not having any faith. I loved him and his attitude against sin and sickness. In fact, the stories had not been enough to really tell me what the man was like, nor can any book written about him do Smith Wigglesworth justice.

After such a great faith-filled life, I have always thought that one woman's unbelief took the heart out of him so that he died early. It happened when Wigglesworth was asked to speak at the funeral of a very close friend he had known for many years.

Wigglesworth was eighty-eight by that time. As he climbed the steps to the auditorium where the funeral was being held, he met a young lady whom he recognized. He said, "Hello. How are you? I prayed for your mother once. She had cancer. Is she healed?"

The woman said, "No, your prayers made her worse." Then she turned and walked away.

Wigglesworth went on into what was called the vestry, the waiting area for the preachers who were to speak. There, before a warm fire, he sat down at a little plain table that had no cloth on it. He put his elbow up onto the table and began to weep. The abrupt words of that young woman regarding his faith in God and his prayers hurt him so deeply that I believe his spirit left his body. He went home to be with the Lord.

Someone came into the vestry in a few minutes and said, "Mr. Wigglesworth, it's time for you to speak now."

He was sitting at the table with his hand still up against his face and his elbow on the table. He had not moved one bit. They shook him and could tell that his body already was getting cold.

I cannot blame the young woman too much, because if you do not have faith, we cannot blame you for it. But I believe that, in reality, this woman's unbelief shortened the life of a great man. Some thought it was climbing the steep stairs to the chapel in the cold and then coming into a very warm room, but I think it was a sudden blow to the heart.

He might have lived several more years and healed thousands more people had it not been for the heartbreak caused by a little woman who told him his prayers for her mother were ineffective.

Wigglesworth told me that I would see the last colossal move of the Holy Spirit. I believe it is beginning to happen now. I will move into any channel God wants me to move. I will be anything He wants me to be. I am ready to get out of this groove into another groove. I believe the words Smith spoke over me the last time I saw him *will* come true.

24

Lilian Barbara Yeomans:
She Mixed Medicine
and Divine Healing
(1861-1942)

I had a strong relationship with Dr. Lilian Yeomans, a medical doctor turned "faith healer."

When I first went to California following Howard Carter, she heard about me and sent word for me to visit her. I was twenty, and she looked to be about sixty-five. At my age today, I would consider her "a young chick." Her countenance was marked with strength and determination.

She had a little square rug in her living room, and when I got there, she said to me, "Kneel down there."

I had glanced into the next room where a heaped up plate of fried chicken was visible on the dining room table. Now you cannot get a preacher to kneel down when fried chicken is before him. He would rather sit down!

However, I was a visitor in her home, and there for the first time, so I felt I had to obey and kneel down. Then she came and laid her hands on me. But she did not touch me lightly; she caught hold of my shoulders and shook me.

If she had been a man, I might have said, "Stop!" But I couldn't stop a woman, so I just took it.

She began to talk, "You amount to something. You be a student. And when you go around the world. . . ," and she went on and on with prayer and advice.

I knelt there thinking, "When is this going to be over with?"

Spiritual blessings sometimes come hard. Finally, she let me up, and we went to the table and had a good dinner together. I stayed two or three hours afterwards, and we talked about the things of God.

I assumed that would be the only time I would see her, because I got on the boat and left. However, about three years later, I came back to the States and was invited to preach in Minneapolis. When I got there, I found that I was preaching with Dr. Yeomans.

She said, "Hi, Skipper!"

That kind of threw me. You might expect a young girl to talk to you like that, but not an older woman. However, like Lillian Trasher, she remained young inside all of her life.

When I was through preaching that night, she said, "Pretty good preaching! You did better than when I last saw you."

And I said, "Thank you."

Then she said, "Let's go out on the town," and when I asked where were we going, she replied, "Let's go get a hamburger."

Two or three other preachers went with us, and she was the life of the party. She began to talk of what faith really is. She talked about the walk of faith, the power of faith, and how God heals.

Then she turned to me and said, "You know, that prayer of mine worked, didn't it?"

Finally, after watching her in amazement, I asked, "Where do you get all that vitality?"

She looked at me very sweetly, and said simply, "From Jesus."

I said, "That is what I want. I want vitality like that."

Even into her eighties, she wrote books and went from city to city in crusades. She was a very effective witness for the Lord Jesus.

Meeting a pioneer like her made me feel real good. When the mouth of a true pioneer opens, life comes out, not just words.

A Rough Beginning for a Pioneer

Dr. Yeomans was another Canadian turned American. She was the oldest of three daughters born in Calgary, Alberta, to parents who were both medical doctors. During the Civil War, and when she was just a toddler, her parents moved to the States, where her father served as a surgeon in the United States Army.

After graduating from the University of Michigan with a medical degree, one of the first women to do so, she returned to Canada to go into practice with her mother, Amelia Le Sueur Yeomans, who was a physician as well as a surgeon.

However, Lilian Yeomans was what you might call "a driving woman," or in today's teminology, "a Type-A personality." It was "go, go, go" with her all of the time, and she took on a heavy medical practice. In order to keep up with the work and stay out of stress, she fell back on drugs such as morphine and chloral hydrate.

Once she realized that she was addicted, she tried every known cure, ending up in a sanitorium. After that, she went to New York City, where she tried to gain a cure through Christian Science practitioners. However, this also failed.

Finally, she began to read the Bible and to learn about sanctification. She did receive healing in 1898 through the ministry of John Alexander Dowie. Immersed in the holiness movement of the late nineteenth century, she believed that she had received a "crisis experience" of sanctification in 1907.

Interestingly enough, she spoke in tongues the same night. She wrote a series of letters to her mother over the next few months describing in detail her understanding of sanctification and the baptism of the Holy Spirit. These later were published as *Pentecostal Letters.*

Her mother sought for this infilling and received it in 1908. Dr. Yeomans evangelized all over the United States and Canada, particularly attempting to pioneer Pentecostalism in Alberta.

When I met her, she had been for some years settled in California. She was teaching classes on divine healing and church history at Aimee Semple McPherson's L.I.F.E. Bible College. She continued to write books that were published between the time she was sixty-five and the time she was eighty.

She was still evangelizing at eighty years of age. She died almost a year to the day after Pearl Harbor and was buried in the famous Los Angeles-area cemetery, Forest Lawn, along with movie stars and other celebrities. She never married. The love of her life was the Lord Jesus Christ.

Part Three
Conclusion

Moving With the Last Blaze of Glory!

And these all, having obtained a good report through faith . . . .

Hebrews 11:39

The pioneers of the Full Gospel movement have all obtained a good report through faith at this point. All of them are now part of that "great cloud of witnesses" in heaven.

If there is anything that I desire for my life, it is that at the end of it I shall have a good report through faith.

A good report means that something unusual was accomplished.

A good report means that a person has kept pace with what God was doing.

Beginning in 1900 and going through the end of this century mark the last days, I believe. In this period of time, every modern convenience has come into being.

The whole world traveled by horse and wagon or carriages when this century was born; now we travel in super jets.

The whole world depended on word of mouth or the postal service in 1900; now we can telephone or fax anywhere on the planet.

These and many other things have come to pass in the lifetime of my parents and in my lifetime. I believe we are living in the finality of the last days.

If the first outpouring of the Spirit was moderate, then God is going to give a double portion as "the latter rain." We will have what the apostles had and what we have at the same time. I believe God is going to double the glory, double the anointing, and double the power.

Zechariah 10:1 tells us:

> Ask ye of the Lord rain in the time of the latter rain; so the Lord shall make bright clouds, and give them showers of rain, to every one grass in the field.

We are to ask the Lord for special rain in the time of the latter rain. And James 5:7 says:

> Be patient therefore, brethren, unto the coming of the Lord. Behold, the husbandman waiteth for the precious fruit of the earth, and hath long patience for it, until he receive the early and latter rain.

We are not to quit, we are not to slow down, but we are to be patient unto the coming of the Lord. The difference between the early rain and the latter rain is that the early rain began on the day of Pentecost some two thousand years ago. It was never withdrawn from the face of the earth, but continued through the centuries until we hit the twentieth century. At the termination of the last century, we had a transition period which is related to the early and latter rain.

Men like Jesse Smith, Billy Sunday and Stephen and George Jeffreys of England, all whom I met personally, opened up something that was new. I thought maybe Dwight L. Moody would be the focal point of the end of the early rain.

When I was in a prayer meeting in Liverpool, England, I was speaking in tongues and an older man moved closer to me and asked, "Can you do that all the time?"

I said, "Yes, as the Spirit moves, I can."

He said, "I was in this city with Dwight L. Moody. As I knelt in prayer with him, he did the same thing you are doing. He spoke in some words that I could not understand."

It is possible that Dwight L. Moody, who aroused the American and British nations at the termination of the old century, finished off the early rain?

At this dramatic moment, our world is plowing through the tenth decade of this century. Almost two thousand years are completed since the Lord Jesus came out of His grave to proclaim that all power had been given to Him in heaven and in earth.

The majority of people throughout Church history never move beyond their first blessing from God — the salvation experience. When John Wesley began to preach sanctification — the cleaning up and discipline of your life — many denominations did not even look around.

They said, "We've already got it all."

Once the average believer gets in a groove, that is exactly where he or she dies. We are creatures of habit. We move ahead in almost everything except God. I think the primary reason is because the devil does not want us to move forward.

In the Bible, the scribes and Pharisees and the Sadducees had their own little cliques. They were in their own little ruts and were determined to stay there until they died. The only thing they ever agreed on was to get rid of Jesus.

People are interesting. They want the latest model car, the latest suit and dress fashions, the nicest food, and the very finest of everything, but when it comes to religion, they do not care. Any old church will do.

God can do something new, and people will say, "Must be fanatics!"

If God does a new thing, I believe it is time to look into what He is doing and move with Him.

In Acts 19, we are told that Paul went to Ephesus. He walked into a church with only twelve people in it. They were having it rough. They could not afford a preacher with only twelve people. Paul found out the twelve had been baptized by John the Baptist, who had his head cut off twenty years earlier. They followed a headless man for twenty years.

Paul began to preach Jesus to them — and they listened. They burned their idols — worth fifty thousand pieces of silver. (One piece of silver was one day's pay at the time.) (Acts 19:19.) That is called revival! They got out of the past groove and into the next one.

People will praise you for buying a new Lincoln, but they will curse you for receiving the Holy Ghost and allowing the gifts of the Spirit to operate through you as the Spirit wills. I believe God has some new things.

Christians Are Not Exempt From Resisting Change

As far as I know, in all of history no denomination ever made a radical change. People can make a change, but denominations rarely do. One of the reasons is because the leaders of a denomination would be embarrassed if people found out they did not know everything about God already.

Jesus was despised because He brought change, a true return to the Word of God in certain areas where they had moved into tradition. When Jesus showed up the religious leaders with new power and blessings, they had a fit! They did not know what to do with Him, except to say, "Kill Him."

In 1900, evangelicals were saying, "Give us revival for the new century."

God sent the Biblical revival of the Holy Spirit from the second chapter of Acts, and the very people who prayed for revival called it "fanaticism."

In the beginning of every revival, the poor and the humble are the ones who receive it first. They do not have anything to lose. It is the same all over the world.

When this revival came at the turn of the century, the new leaders began to preach four things: salvation, water baptism, the infilling of the Holy Spirit, and the second coming of Jesus Christ. These four cardinal truths built the Full Gospel movement on the face of the whole earth.

I began preaching in 1930, when the societies and the cultures of nations were undergoing changes. It was not just the Depression that brought people to Jesus. It was the teachings on endtime prophecy. If you could not teach prophecy, you did not draw a lot of people. Many preachers could not move from the four doctrines of Pentecost into prophecy.

As a young man, I began to learn to move with the times — to move with God. During the Depression, millions of people got saved for two reasons: The troubled economy drove them to God, and the prophecies scared them to God. Many of the messages made you think Jesus was coming at six the next morning!

In our church in Mobile, Alabama, where my parents had moved, a deacon got up one time and said, "On New Year's Eve at 11 P.M., I will come back again, thus saith the Lord Jesus Christ."

Everyone was scared. I was a little shaken because I was not grown yet. When that evening came, the house was packed full of people. I was underneath the seat watching and scared, because I knew I was not ready.

Our whole church was waiting. Three minutes before the hour, the same deacon got up and said, "Thus saith the Lord. I've just changed My mind!"

I wanted to get a ball bat and hit him! Do not think "flaky" prophets and "screwball" Christians are something new! We have had them around for a long time. On the other hand, we must not despise the genuine operation of the gift of prophecy.

After World War II, the Latter Rain movement broke out. It broke out in Canada first, then moved down into Detroit into an Assembly of God church. I went to that church two or three times a year. They were blessed, happy, rejoicing and dancing, but a major denomination's headquarters came against the Latter Rain movement and closed their churches.

It was a gift of prophecy movement, and almost everyone was against it. At that time, they were studying "Bible prophecy," but no one was prophesying. If you prophesy alone, you seem a "screwball" whether you are or not. Although I was a young man, I was grieved because of the way the Holy Spirit was quenched in that move. You see, I am not afraid of wildfire. I know how to put a cover over it. But I am afraid of icebergs!

If the Full Gospel denominations had accepted the Latter Rain movement, they would have enlisted hundreds of thousands of new members because it was the breath of God.

It was a little fanatical in some places, but it could have been corrected by the leaders loving people and teaching them rather than scolding and beating them down. They were accused of being full of the devil. But God in His great mercy, almost simultaneously, raised up the Healing revival.

I had just built a church seating a thousand people, but I only had about three hundred. Evangelist Rex Humbard walked in with thirteen members of his family and asked if he could hold a healing meeting.

Immediately, I said, "Yes."

The building was so new that we did not even have a public address system. We had to raise money for it during the meeting. Before the Humbards were through, we had a hundred and fifty new people. That is like adding about two thousand at a time today.

A few months later, the Humbards brought their tent back to town and another hundred and fifty people were added to our church.

Oral Roberts came to our city, and I was chairman of the meeting. We picked up a few hundred more as a result of his meetings. Other preachers came to town, and more people were added to our church.

Finally, we had the second largest church in the United States. The only one larger was Charles Blair's church in Denver, Colorado. Both of our churches hosted the same speakers.

Then the Pentecostal people declared that none of these preachers belonged to them. They threw them out — and I was among them! When God gave us a new blessing, the old skin could not hold the new wine!

I went to the Philippines and a hundred and fifty thousand people were saved. Oral Roberts came, and another twenty-five thousand were saved in one week. Gordon Lindsay came and nearly thirty thousand more were saved until the whole country was reeling with revival.

The Healing revival went down, and many of its leaders died. If you study those leaders, you will see that power can be dangerous if it is not held in truth, integrity, and holiness. God requires holiness, and if you do not give Him holiness, He will withdraw His presence from you.

I was in the middle of the Healing revival, just as I was in the middle of the Latter Rain movement, the Prophetic revival and the Full Gospel revival.

God in His mercy started another revival — the Charismatic revival. As far as I can tell, it began with the Full Gospel Business Men's Fellowship International, which released the Holy Spirit into denominations. It was delightful.

Then articles were written indicating that there was a drastic difference between being a Pentecostal and being a Charismatic.

Both groups spoke in tongues.

Both believed in the Holy Spirit.

Both believed that Jesus was going to come soon.

Yet barriers were again raised to keep Charismatics out of certain groups.

My church in South Bend today is made up of Catholics, Baptists, Methodists, Presbyterians, Mennonites, Amish — people from many denominations — all loving Jesus together.

Throughout the earth, millions of people were blessed through the Charismatic revival, and then it began to die. As it subsided, God did something else.

He raised up two Texans — Kenneth E. Hagin and under him Kenneth Copeland — and said, "The Word is true. You call it to be true. Teach My people faith."

Many people began to call their teachings "hyper-faith." Again, we could have all moved together in what was called the Word of Faith movement. Yet it has not happened.

We do not have any aspirin tablets in my house. Some Christians' houses could be turned into drugstores because they have so much medicine in their cabinets and keep adding more drugs. We raised our sons without any medicine.

Were any of them ever sick? Certainly, we were, but we laid hands on them, prayed for them, and they got well. We have been tested and tried, and the Word of God is true. As long as I have lived, I never thought anybody would say something derogatory about faith and the Word — the two things we need most — but it has happened.

In every move of God, His people out of the last move have resisted the new one the hardest. Human beings basically do not like change, and Christians are not exempt. Most of us resist change as long as we can.

Spiritual Revolution Is on the Way

Now, I believe the greatest spiritual revolution in the history of the world is about to take place. I am not sure all Christians will be in on it, because it might be too "radical." It may be too "off-beat." Preachers may not look dignified. The gifts of the Spirit will function mightily, moving governments and frightening political leaders. God's Church will come alive just before Jesus comes.

There will be some mainline denominational people who cannot bridge the gap any more than they did in the past.

There will be some Pentecostals and Charismatics who cannot bridge the gap.

There will be some Word of Faith leaders who cannot bridge the gap.

People will say, "That's too far for me to jump from where I am. I'm going to stick it out right here. I'm comfortable where I am."

That is the reason people in other moves of God did not go with the flow of the Holy Spirit. They stayed where they were comfortable.

I have asked God many times, "Please do not do anything while I am alive unless You let me be a part of it."

I promise you, when a new thrust of the Spirit comes, I will not criticize it. I will not find fault with it. I will just receive it and accept it. For those in it who need help, I will try to teach them to get on the right track to be what God wants them to be. Someone needs to be there to hold it together, to love the people, to forgive the little things that are not right.

I believe we are on the verge of a spontaneous move of God. No one has a corner on the blessings of God. The only one who can eliminate you from the blessings of God is yourself. Many of you reading this book will be here when Jesus comes, so you will want to be in the last blaze of glory! Do not expect your denomination or even your church to come with you, but do not curse them if they will not. Do not judge them and call them names. Just move with God yourself.

No organized group ever moved into a new revelation — only individuals do. Organizations come later, when enough individuals have received the new move. Be a person who moves with God wherever He wants you to be.

Keep your heart open and say, "I will be a recipient of whatever You give, Lord."

In more than sixty years of ministry, I have never been sidelined with some stupid doctrine. I never budged in any direction. I believe and teach now what I did when I was a teenager — the same gospel, the same truth, the same anointing, the same power. I am not afraid of anything the devil does.

If something is not right, you can say, "You aren't right according to the Bible. Line yourself up with the Bible or keep your mouth shut."

Very simple! If you will stand that way, you will always abide in truth.

I have been constantly in God's blessing every day of my life. You cannot retire from a blessing. If you are a healing preacher, and you stop going to healing meetings for about ten years then think you're going to jump back in and do the same thing, forget it! You will be as a tinkling cymbal, an empty drum. If you want God's blessings, you have to follow Him constantly.

I have preached for some of the great pioneers when their properties were being taken away.

I encouraged them, "It does not matter about the property. God will give you another piece of property. Just stick with the blessings of God."

Jesus is coming soon. Let us fill the earth with His praises. The more fanatical we are, the greater impact we are going to make on this generation. When people see that we are sincere to the core and not playing with religion, they will believe in us.

I believe the great athletic coliseums are not for football and baseball. They are for the last big breath of God! With the great breath of God that is coming, no one is going to get tired. We are going to flow in the dynamics of the supernatural.

You will find from studying the history of Israel and Judah that God blesses by generations. We need a new generation today, and I can see it beginning. We have some of the strongest young men preaching the gospel today that we have ever had.

These young leaders must watch out, however, for the same pitfalls that brought down some of the leaders of past movements: power (pride and ambition), money, and sex.

It is so easy to get into pride when God blesses your ministry and to take too much of the credit.

It is so easy to get your mind on material gain. Ministers must be givers, not mostly receivers. In accumulation, there comes an awful thing called *greed*. In the "lust of the eyes" for possessions, you can lose your relationship for God.

It is so easy to be enticed into an illicit relationship. Most of those whom I know who have fallen into adultery tell me they never intended to do it. The pastor has become such an idol that having sex with him would be the greatest achievement in the lives of a minimum of ten women out of a church of five hundred people. Most preachers cannot imagine how many women get bowled over by just shaking the preacher's hand.

"I shook his hand! He shook my hand! I felt the blood flowing through his hand into mine."

That is the wrong attitude. Preachers are servants of God and servants of the people. They are not great. Only God is great. Joseph in the Bible is a great example for a preacher to follow.

I have tried to use him as an example in my counseling with women. I have no couches in my office. I have four very straight chairs. If a woman wants counseling and cannot bring her husband, I always have had my wife or my secretary sit in while she tells her story.

However, the lessons I have learned from the first spiritual pioneers — those in the Bible — would make more than another book. In this one, I have tried to show what the pioneers of the Pentecostal movement have meant to me. I have tried to show some of the lessons I have learned from them: integrity, organization, humility, and how to handle the power of God, among other things.

When I die, an era will be over, because it seems I am like a bridge overlapping all of the moves of this century. However, I hope to be alive when not just an era, but all of time will be over. I am convinced that I will at least see this last great revival. I would hope that everyone who reads this will pray with me for the manifestation in its fullness of the "latter rain."

Bibliography

Assemblies of God Archives, 1445 Boonville Avenue, Springfield, Missouri 65802.

Assemblies of God Heritage, "A Church Grows in Chile Because Willis Hoover Took a Stand," Vol. 8, #3, Fall 1988.

Autobiography of Peter Christopher Nelson, unpublished, Assemblies of God Archives.

Barratt, Thomas Ball, *When the Fire Fell*.

Blumhofer, Edith, *The Assemblies of God*, Vol. I, (Springfield: Gospel Publishing House, 1988.)

Brumback, Carl H., *Suddenly . . . From Heaven*.

Burgess, S.M., McGee, G.B., and Alexander, P.H. *Dictionary of Pentecostal and Charismatic Movements* (Grand Rapids: Zondervan Publishing House, 1988. Copyright by the authors.)

Crouch, Philip, *Why They Called Her the Greatest Woman in Egypt*, (Springfield: *Assemblies of God Heritage*, Winter 1984, 1985).

Glad Tidings Herald, Vol. 27, #1, May 1948, New York.

Hollenweger, W.J., *The Pentecostals* (Minneapolis: Augusburg Publishing House, 1972. Translation Copyright SCM Press Ltd.)

Salter, James, "Called to the Congo" (February 1948), "Pioneering for Christ in the Congo, "In God's Hands," (March 1936) The Pentecostal Evangel; "A Life Given Back for the Heathen," *The Latter Rain Evangel*, March 1924.

Sumrall, Lester, *The Nile Mother*, (South Bend: World Harvest Press, 1974).

Ward, C.M. *Elder A.G. Ward — Intimate Glimpses of My Father's Life*, (Springfield: Assemblies of God, 1955.)

Whittaker, Colin C., *Seven Pentecostal Pioneers*, (Springfield: Gospel Publishing House, 1983).

Zimmerman, Thomas F., *Lewi Pethrus — A Leader Ahead of His Times, A Tribute to Lewi Pethrus*, Assembly of God Archives.

Dr. Lester Sumrall is founder and chairman of a worldwide missionary outreach, The Lester Sumrall Evangelistic Association (LeSEA). Respected throughout the world as a missionary statesman, Dr. Sumrall has raised up churches and taught the Word of God for more than sixty years. In addition, he  maintains headquarters for LeSEA Global and LeSEA Broadcasting (international radio and television) in South Bend, Indiana, where he pastors Christian Center Cathedral of Praise. His three married sons, Frank, Stephen, and Peter also are involved in the ministry.

Dr. Sumrall, a prolific author, has written more than 110 books and teaching syllabi. In addition to his writing, he is founder and president of World Harvest Bible College and is host on the television programs, "LeSEA Alive" and "The Lester Sumrall Teaching Series."

A powerful and dynamic speaker, Dr. Sumrall ministers God's message with authority and takes advantage of electronic media to reach the world today. He founded LeSEA Broadcasting, Inc., which owns and operates eight television stations in the following cities:

WHMB TV-40 Indianapolis, Indiana

WHME TV-46 South Bend, Indiana

KWHB TV-47 Tulsa, Oklahoma

KWHE TV-14 Honolulu, Hawaii

WHKE TV-55 Kenosha, Wisconsin

KWHD TV-53 Denver, Colorado

KWHH TV-14 Hilo, Hawaii

K21AG TV-21 Maui, Hawaii

A recent outreach to the world's hungry has thrust Dr. Sumrall into a new dimension of showing compassion to the far corners of the earth in response to our Lord's command to "feed the hungry." Called the End Time Joseph Program to Feed the Hungry, Dr. Sumrall is enlisting worldwide pastor-to-pastor support of this program. It is his belief that government alone should not shoulder the responsibility of caring for the world's homeless, hungry, and needy, but that the Church is to be a responsible vehicle of Christ to suffering humanity.

To receive Lester Sumrall's monthly
magazine, *World Harvest*, write:

Lester Sumrall
P. O. Box 12
South Bend, Indiana 46624

*Please include your prayer requests
and comments when you write.*

Receive the Sword
at Lester Sumrall's World Harvest Bible College.
For a free catalog about WHBC
or correspondence studies, write:

World Harvest Bible College
P. O. Box 12
South Bend, Indiana 46624

Also by Lester Sumrall

Be Bold and Walk Tall

Courage to Conquer

Demons — The Answer Book

Faith to Change the World

The Names of God

Victory and Dominion Over Fear

101 Questions and Answers on Demon Powers

Living Free

Miracles Don't Just Happen

Run With the Vision

These and other titles
by Lester Sumrall are
available from your local bookstore.

Harrison House

Tulsa, Oklahoma 74153

In Canada contact: Word Alive, P.O. Box 670
Niverville, Manitoba CANADA ROA 1EO

The Harrison House Vision

Proclaiming the truth and the power
Of the Gospel of Jesus Christ
With excellence.

Challenging Christians to
Live victoriously,
Grow spiritually,
Know God intimately.